James Pollard

A study in municipal government

the corporation of Berlin

James Pollard

A study in municipal government
the corporation of Berlin

ISBN/EAN: 9783743313743

Manufactured in Europe, USA, Canada, Australia, Japa

Cover: Foto ©ninafisch / pixelio.de

Manufactured and distributed by brebook publishing software (www.brebook.com)

James Pollard

A study in municipal government

CONTENTS.

CHAP.		PAGE
I.	MUNICIPAL DEPARTMENTS,	3
II.	WATER AND GAS,	17
III.	SANITATION—DRAINAGE—STREET-CLEANING,	33
IV.	DOMESTIC SANITATION—MEAT INSPECTION,	51
V.	PUBLIC HOSPITALS—CONVALESCENT HOMES,	69
VI.	ADMINISTRATION FOR RELIEF OF THE POOR,	87
VII.	EDUCATION AND THE COMMON SCHOOLS,	105
VIII.	PUBLIC WORKS—FREE LIBRARY—FIRE-BRIGADE,	125
IX.	POLICE—TREASURY—POWERS OF CORPORATION,	145
	INDEX,	161

CHAPTER I.

MUNICIPAL DEPARTMENTS.

Rapid development of Berlin—Its present importance—Constitution of the Corporation — Offices of Ober Bürgermeister, Bürgermeister, Magistrate, and Town Councillor—Functions of the Magistracy and Town Council—Paid and unpaid magistrates—Administrative departments and committees—Corporation supervision in all institutions affecting public wellbeing—City finance—Annual charges—Local rates—Methods of raising rates—Annual departmental reports—Berlin municipal Brown-book.

THE chief city of the German empire is now within easy reach of any part of Great Britain. By the Queenborough-Flushing route, the traveller covers the distance from London in twenty-four hours, while from Edinburgh or Dublin he may do so within thirty-six hours. He may, this morning, be filling his mind with the historic associations of Holyrood or College Green, and to-morrow night be strolling by Frederick the Great's statue in Unter den Linden. And, however uninviting Berlin may have been twenty years ago, before the extraordinary development which, in all departments of its civic administration, it has made within that period, it may be safely said that there is now no city in Europe which presents so many interesting features to the student of municipal government. It has not, indeed, the historic interest of the old free towns of Hamburg, Bremen, Lübeck, or Frankfort; still less can it in this respect compare with the more ancient cities beyond the Rhine and the Alps. Long before it played any part in the life of the German people, small towns like Wittenberg, Erfurt, and Eisenach were shaping the destinies of the nation. But Berlin had the distinction of being made the capital of the Hohenzollerns; and it has followed their fortunes and shared their fame. Through many vicissitudes the little double town of Berlin-Kölln struggled to establish itself on the sluggish Spree. Its far-sighted traders saw that, though their town was placed in the midst of an arid plain, their river afforded them a highway to the fruitful valleys of the Elbe and the Oder, and would enable them to join the commerce of Poland and Eastern Europe with that of the Baltic and the Northern Sea. At the close of the Thirty Years' War the town did not number more than 6000 inhabitants, but from that time it grew in size and importance. It was, however, only in the time of Frederick the Great that Berlin became one of the foremost capitals of Europe. At the death of Frederick, in 1786, the population of the city was 145,000, while at the beginning of the present century it was 172,000. Since 1800 its growth has been marvellously rapid. At the present time the population is no less than 1,635,000. Berlin has become the greatest manufacturing and industrial centre on the Continent. The trade carried on its river and canals is greater even than the trade of the Rhine, and its money and grain markets are among the greatest in Europe. No city in the eastern hemisphere has within so short a period shown such wonderful expansion; it is only among the cities of the New World that a parallel can be found. At the present moment a project is under serious consideration, and it appears to meet with favour, to extend the boundaries of the city to a radius of nearly ten miles from the present centre, the point at which the Friedrich Strasse intersects the Unter den Linden. If this were done, the population would number three millions, and Berlin would stand second only to London among the capitals of the world. As things are, the population is increasing at the rate of nearly forty thousand a-year.

Since the war with France the whole municipal organisation has undergone such a revision as the enormous growth of the city called for. With admirable thoroughness the work of improvement and reform has been carried on in every department. It is the object of the present study to show to what attainments these reforms have reached. It may be hoped that, if the narrative affords some examples that may be worthy of imitation by municipalities in this country, town councillors and others concerned in various branches of local government may not be above learning what may prove useful in their own administration, even though the examples are taken from Germany.

The Corporation of Berlin (*Berliner Gemeinde Verwaltung*) is presided over by a chief mayor (*Ober Bürgermeister*) and a mayor (*Bürgermeister*), like the Chairman and Deputy-Chairman of the London County Council. Both are paid offices, the first carrying a salary of £1500, and the second £900 per annum. The choice lies in both cases with the Town Council, who are not limited to members of their own body, nor even to citizens of Berlin. Recently the office of Ober Bürgermeister became vacant through the death of Herr von Forckenbeck, and one of the candidates spoken of for the vacancy was the Bürgermeister of Danzig, whose success as an administrator is widely known in Germany. The choice of the Town Council (*Stadtverordneter Versammlung*) for both offices is, however, subject to the approval of the Emperor as King of Prussia, who may, without reason assigned, veto the election of any one who is not after his own mind. But the royal veto is exercised in a generous manner, for Herr Zelle, who has just been appointed, is a Liberal. There is a Magistracy (*Magistrat*) of thirty members chosen by the Town Council, but each magistrate must be approved by the Chief President (*Ober-Präsident*) or Civil Governor of the province of Brandenburg, who has his official residence in the city. The magistrates do not sit as members of council, but in a chamber of their own; and they alone have the power to initiate civic legislation, to elaborate its details, and finally to pass laws for the government of the city. The Town Council consists of 126 members (*Stadtverordneten*), elected from various districts or wards of the city by manhood suffrage, in the same manner as representatives are chosen for the Prussian Parliament. The Town Council has no legislative functions, but may make representations to the Magistracy on matters which seem to call for legislation; the latter body, if it approve, proceeds in the manner described with whatever measures may be needful to carry out the desired object. Of the thirty magistrates, fifteen are expected to devote their whole time to the service of the town, and are paid salaries ranging from 7000 to 15,000 marks, or about £350 to £750 per annum. In one or two special cases the salary may reach £900. The unpaid magistrates have the same official status as those who are paid; but in the case of the latter it is imperative, whatever other qualifications they may possess, that they shall be well versed in the law of the land and possess a full knowledge of municipal law. The members of the Magistracy are for the most part men who have served for some time as town councillors, and who have shown special aptitude for administrative work. Although the Magistracy and the Town Council in their corporate capacity act independently, and are somewhat in the relative positions of an upper and lower house, yet in the general work of administration, which, as with us, is carried on by committees, their members mingle and have equal votes. There are committees for the various departments: committees for buildings, streets, and roadways, for lighting, cleaning, and water-supply; there are sanitation, drainage, and hospital committees; parks and markets committees; committees for the common schools, the care of the poor, the regulation of the police, and the control of finance. The chairmen (*Vorsitzenden*) of these committees are usually magistrates, and the more important committees have one of the paid magistrates for chairman. It is not only the work of the general management of the city which falls under the charge of the Berlin Corporation, but matters which with us fall under separate administration. For example, the care of the poor, the management of the common schools, the administration of the public hospitals, as well as the water-supply, and, to a large extent, the gas-supply of the city, which in this country are usually under the control of separate boards and trusts, are, in Berlin, all under direct municipal supervision. It must be said that, though such an arrangement seems to centralise large powers in the municipal body, it has very great economic advantages, as we may see by-and-by. It is sufficient, meanwhile, to say that, wherever the Corporation take responsibility, they insist upon obtaining the principal direction of affairs. In all such cases the whole income and expenditure are treated as part of the income and expenditure of the Corporation, and are dealt with in the annual accounts of the city. It is thus possible to obtain a clear view of the whole cost to the inhabitants of all the public departments of the city, whether these are maintained directly out of the taxes levied, or, as in the case of gas, water, and other matters, paid for according to individual requirements.

Berlin has a public debt of about $12\tfrac{1}{2}$ millions sterling. Less than a million of this sum is old debt bearing interest at $4\tfrac{1}{2}$ per cent.; the whole of the other $11\tfrac{1}{2}$ millions bears $3\tfrac{1}{2}$ per cent, which is the annual rate at which the city of Berlin can now easily borrow money. The Corporation expend annually for all the purposes under their control about 80 million marks, or, in round figures, about 4 millions sterling. This expenditure, though apparently large, is in reality considerably less per head of the population than is the expenditure in a city like Edinburgh, and very much less than in most of our large towns, if to our ordinary burgh rates we add all that is expended under our poor and school boards, and in connection with our public hospitals. For ordinary municipal purposes, such as are covered, for example, by the Edinburgh burgh and police rate, now standing at 2s. 1d. per £1 of the assessed rental, the Berliners pay almost exactly the same amount in proportion. But their method of raising their assessments differs from ours in two ways. In the first place, while they raise part of their rates from the rent-roll of the dwellings, no man is assessed upon his rental who pays a lower rent than 200 marks, or, say, £10 per annum. Ratepayers pay on a graduated scale, beginning at 2 per cent. on 200 marks, and rising to $6\frac{1}{2}$ per cent. when the rent exceeds 1000 marks a-year. In the second place, part of the municipal rates is raised by means of a graduated income-tax, beginning with incomes of 660 marks, or £33, per annum. By these two methods the whole sums required for ordinary municipal purposes are levied. But the municipal accounts embrace all other sources of revenue —the rents paid by tramway companies for the use of streets, the surplus profits from the gas and water establishments, the revenues from irrigation fields used by the town for utilisation of sewage, income from markets and slaughter-houses, and so forth.

Each department of the town's service forms the subject of a separate annual report. In this report the whole details of the establishment to which it refers are fully described; attention is called to any new work begun or any development in existing branches of work during the year. Newly sanctioned proposals are set forth, and reasons are given for all extra expenses which have been incurred. All the reports of the different departments are bound into one volume, and issued by the Magistracy with a general report prefixed. In the magisterial report one may see at a glance the general progress of the city and the special matters of municipal interest which may have occurred during the year; while for details one may turn to the reports of the separate establishments. In clearness and fulness of statement it would seem hardly possible to excel the magisterial Brown-book of Berlin (*Verwal-*

tungs - Bericht des Magistrats zu Berlin). The most exacting ratepayer may there satisfy himself regarding the expenditure of every fraction of the rates, and he may judge of the reasons assigned for every fresh item of expenditure. Nor need the dullest town councillor be at a loss for material to enable him to explain to his constituents why this and that piece of work has been undertaken, what it has cost, and what are the benefits which it is expected to yield. The statements of accounts, which, of course, are after the German decimal system, are models of perspicacity and orderliness.

To appreciate fully, however, the methods of civic government now in practice, they must be seen in operation. There is no more profitable way in which a person interested in such matters can spend a holiday in Berlin than by making use of the facilities which are courteously placed at his disposal by the heads of departments there.

WATER AND GAS

CHAPTER II.

WATER AND GAS.

Public debt of Berlin — Redemption of debt — Water-supply — Under public company — Taken over by Corporation — Sale of water by meter — How introduced — Mr Gill's experiments — Success of the Siemens meter — Final adoption of meter system — Tenement dwellings convenient for its use — Favourable results of introduction — Statistics of water-supply — Prevailing cleanliness — Meter system in other German towns — Lighting of Berlin — Gas-supply by Corporation — Lighting of streets — Petroleum light in parks — Statistics of gas supply — Electric light.

WHEN it is stated that the annual expenditure of the city is about four millions sterling, it is to be kept in view that this expenditure includes all that is raised for the support of the common schools, the public hospitals, and the care of the poor. On the other hand, as has been said, the city receives whatever profits are made on the water-supply, on the gas-works under the management of the Corporation, and from sundry other sources. In the 12½ millions of the city's debt are included the capital amounts standing against the various establishments — namely, against gas-works, water-works, drainage-works, cattle-market, slaughter-house, and general markets, and against school and other institution buildings. Nearly the whole of this debt has been incurred in connection with operations sanctioned within the past twenty years. The tendency for the present is towards an increase of the total, through further improvements that are going forward in different departments; but at the same time, an annual sum of about £280,000 is being set aside out of the municipal revenue for the redemption of debt. No doubt a larger sum will be used in this way in proportion as any increase is made to capital expenditure. It may therefore be said that the total present debt of the city is in the way of being wiped off in course of thirty years; and for a city like Berlin, growing in wealth as in many other things, this cannot be regarded as a very unwieldy burden. Indeed, all things considered, Berlin stands, in respect of its total financial obligations, more favourably than Edinburgh, which is by no means one of the most heavily burdened municipalities.

In the matter of its water-supply, the German capital affords many instructive points. Like Edinburgh it was served, till recent years, by a public company. It was not till 1873 that the Corporation took the works under their own control, and great public advantage has followed from the change. The supply is brought from two large lakes—the Tegel to the north-west, and the Müggel to the south-east of the city; the one fed by a tributary of the Spree, and the other by the Spree itself, about nine miles before it reaches the city. It is obvious that, gathered in an extensive plain, this water must necessarily undergo a complete process of filtration before it can be regarded as fit for domestic use. Accordingly, the water-works (*Städtische Wasserwerke*) embrace enormous structures for this purpose, and these have been greatly extended and improved since the water-supply was taken over by the city. As delivered for consumption, the water is of good, wholesome quality, while the sources are regarded as amply sufficient for the wants of the city, even if it continue to grow as rapidly for the next two or three generations. An increased demand will, no doubt, require additional works and filtering stations, but it will not for very many years compel the Corporation to seek new sources of supply. The most noteworthy feature of the subject is that in Berlin the water is now sold to the inhabitants by meter just as gas is sold; and experience has shown that this system has proved a great public benefit. It may, therefore, not be without interest to observe how the meter system has come to be introduced, as well as to note the results which have been obtained.

The company which formerly supplied Berlin had a concession under which it was entitled to charge an assessment of 4 per cent. on the rental in name of water-rate, and it was obliged to maintain an unlimited supply. Its works, however, were constructed only with a view to a moderate growth of the city, and in 1865 it began to find that the demand was growing largely in excess of the supply. It was evident, however, that great waste was going on, and that if this could be properly checked, it would still be possible with the existing works to meet the wants even of a greater number of consumers. To prevent waste was, however, found to be practically impossible unless some self-checking method of distribution could be devised. In such circumstances it occurred to Mr Henry Gill, the manager and engineer of the company—an Englishman, who had been at the head of the water department since 1856, and who, to the great satisfaction of the municipality, has held the same position down to the present date — to suggest the introduction of a meter system. No doubt the increased demand could have been adequately met by the erection of new works to make enlarged use of the sources of water at command. But this would have meant ruin to the company. What was required by the necessities of the case was, not more water, but a proper and reasonable use of that which was available. The history of the company, as Mr Gill himself puts it, was, like the history of water companies in general, the record of an incessant struggle to diminish or prevent waste. The powers which they possessed of house inspection, of prescribing the nature and construction of apparatus for the conveyance and delivery of water, and of even exacting fines for non-compliance with fixed regulations, were all found to be wholly inadequate to prevent the waste which was constantly caused by ignorance and neglect. It was felt that improvement could only be effected by a change in the method of assessing the charges for the water which passed through the service-pipes of the consumers. So long as the rate bore no relation to the quantity of water consumed, and did not depend either on the number of rooms or on the number of water-taps or other appliances, the experience was that there was no inducement to the householder either to use the water economically, or to keep his apparatus in proper repair. In this way the company or the corporation charged with the water-supply always suffers, but in the long-run the loss, whatever it may be, falls on the community. Mr Gill began by proposing a tentative change. Meters were already in use for a few large consumers. It was proposed to select blocks of buildings with the heaviest rentals, and to undertake to serve these with a water-supply adequate to all reasonable requirements, upon a scale somewhat lower than the rate at which the company was entitled to assess under the old system, but to pass the supply through meters upon condition that an extra charge should be made for any excess beyond the supply agreed to. The experiment proved successful. People did not use less water for necessary purposes, for the minimum supply was sufficient in that respect, but to save their pockets they guarded against waste. Gradually the Siemens meter, which was the one selected by the company, was improved, and the system was slowly extended, until its economical advantages to consumers and the department became more widely appreciated. Finally, in 1878, on the recommendation of Mr Gill, the Corporation—which had meanwhile bought up the company—made the system general throughout the city. Almost all Berlin lives in flats; self-contained houses being exceptional. Each house or tenement has an average of four floors, each floor containing two or it may be three separate dwellings. The average number of inhabitants occupying a tenement is about seventy. The meter is situated on the ground floor within the passage leading from the street, and is so placed that it may be readily examined, and yet not easily injured. It is the property of the department, while the apparatus within the house belongs to the proprietor. An annual charge, now reduced to about 6s., is made for the meter. The department holds the proprietor responsible for payment of the whole consumption registered by the meter, and he therefore is vigilant to prevent waste through neglect or deterioration of apparatus. The tenant has nothing directly to do with the rate; the landlord keeps it in view in fixing the rent. As all dwellings are treated in this manner, tenants insist on having complete water, water-closet, and, frequently, bath accommodation. Each house being supplied direct from the main, which affords a constant supply, cisterns are not required. This is a great aid to the sanitary condition of the dwellings. Water-closets are now so general in private dwellings that over head there is one for every nine persons; while there is one bath for every eighty of the population. Besides, Berlin is liberally supplied with large public bathing-places and other sanitary conveniences.

The present works are capable of delivering daily into the city about 150,000 cubic metres, or over 33,000,000 gallons, equal to 20 gallons per head of the population, or one-half of the Edinburgh supply. The actual consumption is, however, only 15 gallons per head. About 3 per cent. of the supply is used for public sanitary purposes. It is to be noted that while the supply per head appears to be comparatively small, the system of serving an average of seventy persons by one meter contributes towards keeping the supply at what is actually necessary, and secures that what one inhabitant may not require in one day his neighbour obtains, and *vice versa*. And it must be said that in the poorer quarters of the town the Berliners appear to make a far more effective use of water in the cleanliness of their persons and dwellings than even Edinburgh can boast. If a more liberal supply should be found to be necessary for the city, the Corporation are quite able to afford additional works. For while the present actual cost of water is only about 4s. per head of the population (in Edinburgh it is 4s. 10d.), they make, after meeting all expenses of maintenance, management, and contribution to redemption of debt, an annual profit of no less than £108,000, or 34 per cent. of their total revenue, while in Edinburgh a surplus of not quite 3 per cent. is obtained. If the Berliners were now paying 4 per cent. on their rental, which they did under their water company for a far less satisfactory supply, their water-rate would amount to 6s. 8d. per head of the population, against the 4s. which they actually pay. They have thus, in the matter of rate, through the water-supply having been taken over by the Corporation, had a favourable experience almost exactly corresponding to that of Edinburgh, while their annual profit by the undertaking is ten times greater.

It used to be said that it was only in a place like Berlin, where tenement dwellings are so universally used, that the meter system of water-supply could be successfully worked. Experience has shown, however, that it can be successfully used in other circumstances, for it has already been adopted by many of the principal towns in Germany, while it is about to be introduced by others.

Although gas-lighting was introduced in London in 1814, Berlin continued the use of oil-lamps for public and domestic lighting till 1827. In that year a strong English company, which had already established gas undertakings in other German towns, obtained a twenty-one years' concession for the gas-supply of Berlin. The Corporation became so satisfied, towards the end of the period, that the growth of the city and the large profits of the company warranted them in starting a gas establishment of their own, that they declined to continue the monopoly. In 1847 they erected gas-works (*Städtische Gasanstalten*) under their own administration. Not to be beaten, the company, which was allowed to continue its business as an independent concern, instantly reduced its price from 10 marks per 1000 English cubic feet to 5 marks, and the latter became the price of the town supply as well. It is unnecessary to relate the competitive struggle between the town and the company. The increase of the population provided ample scope for both, and both are still in friendly rivalry. The municipal undertaking has developed to four times its original size, and now possesses four large works in different quarters of the city. In 1865 the use of English coal in gas manufacture was discontinued, and the coal now used is brought from the mines of Upper and Lower Silesia and of Westphalia, at a cost of about 18s. per English ton. By the introduction of the new method of treating coal-gas with oxygen, the quality of the gas has been much improved, and it yields a light 22 candles strong. Ordinary consumers pay at present about 4s. 8d. per 1000 English cubic feet, but this price includes the cost of public lighting, which is borne by the gas department. No city in Europe, excepting Paris perhaps, is so well lighted at night as Berlin. The authorities believe that with abundance of light crime is diminished and more easily detected. As the gas consumed in public lighting is supplied by the department, the cost is laid on the price charged to general consumers. At the present time it represents about 8d. per 1000 feet of the selling price, so that the net price per 1000 feet is only 4s. for private consumption. When extensions are required to keep pace with the increase of the city, the municipal treasury bears the first cost; but all expenses of maintenance and depreciation, as well as reduction of debt, are borne by the department, which, nevertheless, usually ends its year with a good surplus. Last year the surplus, after meeting all charges, was £250,000, which was passed to the city treasury for general municipal purposes. The output by the city is at present 3800 million cubic feet, while the gas used is within 6.01 per cent. of that quantity—a comparatively low percentage of shortcoming. A somewhat novel practice is carried on by the department in insuring consumers against loss by gas explosion; and in this way a revenue is obtained out of which provision is made for the widows of gas employees who have died in the service of the town. To avoid damage to trees and shrubs by the cutting up of the ground, no gas-pipes are laid in the public gardens, which are lit at night by a system of petroleum lamps, and occasionally by electricity.

With a demand for gas requiring an annual increase of 5 per cent. on the output—an increase exceeding that of the population—the administration regard with complacency the development of the electric light, which is still very far from coming into serious competition with their commodity. So far back as 1883, however, the city granted permission to a public company to lay down an installation of electric light, and the business of the company has shown considerable development. Several of the principal streets, squares, and public buildings are now illuminated by this means; but it is so expensive as to be far beyond the reach of the general consumer. The Corporation, however, keep a sharp eye on its progress; they have taken care not to give the company exclusive rights, and they may be trusted not to hesitate to take the business entirely into their own hands whenever it appears to be for the public advantage that this should be done.

SANITATION, DRAINAGE, AND STREET-CLEANING

CHAPTER III.

SANITATION, DRAINAGE, AND STREET-CLEANING.

Insanitary state of Berlin before 1872—Virchow—His public services to Berlin—His zeal for sanitary reform—Corporation resolved on thorough measures—"Radial" system of drainage—Gathering-tanks—Pumping-stations—Utilisation of sewage—Sewage-fields—Three classes of fields—Cost of works—Results—Cleansing of streets—Removal of street and house refuse—Watering of streets—Public lavatories—The cleansing staff—Clean scavengers.

IN 1871, just after the war with France, with a population already exceeding 800,000, the sanitary condition of Berlin was, with the exception perhaps of the city of Köln, the worst of any city in Germany. Not only was there no proper system of drainage, but the dwellings of the poor were most unhealthy. Until that time, and, indeed, down to recent years, the houses of the poor were either in the basement floors of the tenements, in the cellars, or in the top floors, to which access was obtained by separate staircases from those used by the well-to-do, who occupied the better floors. Three-storey tenements were then common, while now, even in the wealthy quarters of the town, tenements are often five storeys in height. There were then as many as 4565 dwellings in which there was no fireplace, and there were 95,000 which had only one room with a fireplace. Reckoning four persons to a family, there were thus almost half the inhabitants living under such comfortless and unhealthy conditions. This was the state of matters only twenty-one years ago. The mortality of the city was in consequence extremely high.

For the beneficent changes that have been brought about in the sanitation of the city no man is so much entitled to public gratitude as Professor Virchow. He is one of the most industrious of the world's workers. He is celebrated all the world over as the most eminent pathologist of his age; but for five-and-twenty years of the busiest portion of his life he has found time to discharge the duties of a member both of the Landtag and Reichstag, and of the humbler office of town councillor as well. It is in the latter capacity that he has rendered such splendid services to Berlin. In 1872 Virchow presented a report to the Town Council, in which he showed the urgent need there was to grapple with the whole question of sanitary improvement. He demonstrated that, dividing the preceding fifteen years into three periods of five years each, the mortality of the city was advancing in the ratio of 5, 7, 9, so that in a fourth period it would have more than doubled on the first. He also showed that over the same periods the mortality of children under one year was in the ratio of 5, 7, 11, so that it had actually doubled within fifteen years. Of the 27,800 deaths which occurred in 1872, no fewer than 11,136 were of children under one year. This was clearly a state of things which called clamantly for remedial measures of the most thorough kind. The Corporation wisely resolved upon no half measures. They determined to act with energy, and to abolish the evil root and branch.

They appointed a commission to visit the principal cities of France and Great Britain, to collect information on the most effective methods of drainage and the disposal of city refuse. The result was that in 1873 works were commenced which transformed the city in a few years from one of the most unhealthy to one of the safest on the Continent. Not only was the increasing mortality checked, but it has been reduced from over 30 to about 20 per 1000, and the tendency is towards further diminution.

The level nature of the site on which Berlin is built presented great difficulties to the introduction of a perfect system of drainage (*Kanalisation*), but these difficulties have been admirably overcome. The city was divided into five great drainage districts. These have since been subdivided, and there are now twelve in all. A point was chosen at the lowest level in each district as that to which the main drain-channels should converge. These are fed from smaller drains, and these again from soil-pipes leading from the dwellings, so that a perfect vein-system overspreads the whole district and finds its centre in enormous gathering-tanks of 40 feet diameter, placed at the lowest level. The main sewers are built of brick, the smaller pipes are of tile-ware. The cellar dwellings lying too low for drainage purposes were no longer allowed to be used as habitations, while the improved water-supply, already described, greatly aided the general work. It was not enough, however, to gather the liquid sewage into one centre; it had to be disposed of as quickly as it was gathered. Accordingly, at each of the gathering-points there is a great pumping-station, with engines—some of them capable of working up to 176 horse-power—by means of which the sewage is forced through immense pipes to sewage-fields. These fields (*Rieselfelder*) are the property of the Corporation, and are situated at from six to ten miles outside the city, where the sewage is used for irrigating purposes with the most satisfactory results.

These sewage-fields are a most noteworthy feature in the sanitary arrangements of the city. They comprise nearly a dozen separate properties, which were formerly barren heaths, and which have all been bought by the Corporation within the last eighteen years for the special purpose of utilising the town sewage. In the aggregate they cover an area of nearly twenty-two square miles. The sewage is pumped to the highest point upon each estate—about 68 feet above the level at the pumping-stations—where it is discharged into a large tank, corresponding to that from which it has come. From this point it is spread over the whole estate, according to the requirements of different parts, the distribution being effectively regulated by an elaborate system of sluices and watercourses.

At the pumping-stations in the city there are self-acting registers, which record the quantity of water passing through the gathering-tank. Readings of the register are taken four times daily. A heavy rainfall flushing the drains necessitates, of course, a more rapid evacuation of the tanks, and this is simply and readily accomplished by increasing the forcing power of the engines. Before passing into the tank, the water is led through iron nettings with one-inch apertures, and all solid matter — wood, paper, straw, and such things—is gathered apart, to be carted away to canal barges. By these it is conveyed, with ashes, house-refuse, and street-sweepings, to be used on farm-land at a distance from the city. At the receiving-tank on each estate there is also a self-acting register; and by a simple arrangement the inspector of the estate may tell at any hour of the day or night at what point the water stands. During the day a flag, and during the night a bright lantern, rises or falls on a flag-staff as the volume of water in the tank is greater or less; thus the risk of overflow is obviated, and the inspector sitting in his office, it may be a couple of miles away, is able to order and regulate the outflow at will.

The sewage-fields are divided into three kinds: first, those which have grown richest in soil are used as fruit-orchards, and let out to market-gardeners, who supply the fruit-markets of Berlin; second, those which are rich enough to bear turnips, potatoes, and grain crops are partly let out to tenants, and partly managed by the Corporation; and third, those still growing grass are wholly in the hands of the Corporation, who sell the grass to cow-feeders and others. As many as five crops of grass are obtained in a season from the last-mentioned fields. One of the estates which has been longest in use now yields a profit of about 3 per cent. on the cost of the land and irrigation works, after payment of all working expenses, renewals, and upkeep. The others promise to show results at least as satisfactory in course of time. According to the last published accounts, the gross yearly cost for the maintenance of the drainage system, including the interest upon and part payment for redemption of capital, was 13,210,567 marks. The ordinary working and upkeep of the machinery cost 662,069, working and maintenance of the fields 1,788,765, and general maintenance of drains and fittings 218,942 marks. By far the greater part of the expenditure is at present spent in extending the *Radial system* (as the city drainage system is called) in new streets, and the purchase and laying out of new fields. The ordinary receipts from the letting and sale of produce from the sewage-fields were last year 1,961,746 marks. The total debt incurred by the city on these works and fields amounts to 78,640,000 marks; but the fields themselves are yearly increasing in value, and must represent a very large asset against the original cost. It may be mentioned that the town is doing a considerable trade in cow-feeding and cattle-raising on these estates. The net annual cost to the city in this department, including interest and reduction of debt, is stated at little over 5,500,000 marks, or, say, £276,000; while the net cost of street cleaning and lighting is stated at 2,486,000 marks, or £124,300. The net total cost of drainage, cleaning, and lighting is therefore £400,000, which, in proportion to the population, corresponds favourably with most large towns in this country.

The cleaning and watering of the streets (*Strassenreinigungswesen*) is now carried out in the same systematic and efficient manner that characterises all the municipal departments. Upwards of thirty miles of street are laid down in asphalt, which greatly facilitates the cleaning.

For the purposes of this department the city is laid out in twenty-three separate districts. One director is over all, while each district has a separate overseer, and is subdivided into minor districts, with a foreman over each. The department employs 662 men, whose wages average 21 marks per week, and 120 lads from fourteen to seventeen years of age, with a weekly wage of from 9 to 16 marks. The carting of house and street refuse is done by contractors, who convey the material to canal-boats on the Spree for the purpose of being conveyed to farms, where it is sold for what it may bring. For the right of using a one-horse cart the contractors pay from one to one and a half mark, for a two-horse cart two marks; and this is the whole revenue the town derives from this source. These carts are made light but strong. There are no refuse-destructors in Berlin. The soil of the surrounding country is so poor that the city refuse is a welcome aid to its cultivation.

The street-sweepers work in relays—there is a day and night shift of twelve hours each, with intervals for meals. In summer, especially during the period of extra street-watering, the day shift frequently works one hour and a half longer. The street-sweepings are collected into shoots or gullies, which are placed along the streets at intervals of 65 yards. Into these gullies the water-courses also run, the water passing into the drains by connecting pipes, the solid matter sinking to the bottom, from which it is emptied at night, and carted away by the contractors. The ventilation of the drains is effected by traps, also placed at regular intervals of about 80 yards along the roadway. These traps serve as man-holes for the proper inspection of the drains. Large use is made of disinfectants, which, particularly in warm weather, are liberally poured into the gullies and drains. The street-sweeping is almost entirely performed at night. Brushing and scraping machines drawn by horses turn out half an hour before midnight, and carry on their operations till about six in the morning. It is at night, too, that ashes and house-refuse, as well as the emptyings of the street gullies, are carried off by the contractors' carts. In very frosty weather the sweeping is delayed till the early hours of morning. Each district has a separate depot, where the men meet, and the cleaning implements are deposited. During the day there is a constant staff of 80 men in fine weather, and 100 in dirty weather, employed in the streets to see to the condition of the water-channels — more especially during heavy rains — to prevent stoppage in the drain inlets and gullies, to scatter sand on the asphalted roadways during frost, and to supervise the public conveniences.

At suitable places in the leading thoroughfares there are public lavatories, some for males, others for females. Each is in charge of an attendant. In most of them one may not only wash and brush up, but have one's boots polished. Such establishments, it is needless to say, are obvious desiderata in any properly managed town. In Berlin they are kept scrupulously clean.

For the purpose of street-watering, hydrants are placed at convenient points throughout the city. As a rule, this operation is only in use from May till September, the other months of the year being wet enough in Berlin. The streets are watered twice or thrice a-day, and in the crowded thoroughfares even more frequently. Each water-cart contains about 250 gallons, and the water department is allowed about 4d. per 1000 gallons for water used on the streets. It is a special duty of the cleaning staff to prevent the hydrants getting frozen in winter. If cholera should reach Berlin during the present epidemic, it will be interesting to compare the effect with visitations of the scourge before the improvements now described were introduced.[1] To fully appreciate the extent and completeness of the change, one must have visited Berlin before and after the introduction. Those who know the city merely as it was in 1872 have only recollections of nauseous smells in the streets, and abominable odours and wofully defective drainage in the houses, and even in the principal hotels. Now all is changed. The most ordinary hotels

---

[1] This passage was written before the recent outbreak of cholera at Hamburg. The almost complete immunity of Berlin, notwithstanding the close proximity of the scourge, is a striking object-lesson on the value of a thorough system of sanitation under wise direction. What would not Hamburg give now to have sooner pursued the same policy as Berlin!

are amply supplied with baths and water-closets of the most recent construction, and the general atmosphere is so sweet that no visitor can have the old dread of carrying off the seeds of typhoid or even typhus as a souvenir.

In connection with this part of municipal work, there is a simple and yet very suggestive matter which strikes the visitor to Berlin who is comparing notes with the state of things at home. It is that the scavengers are all clad in overalls and wide leggings of coarse hempen stuff, which gives them an appearance of tidiness and preserves their ordinary clothes from pollution. With an official cap on his head, a belt round his waist, giving his plain large tunic a somewhat smart appearance, the Berlin scavenger feels that he is a public servant, and that though his occupation may be menial, yet his health and comfort are of some concern to his masters. The municipality take no credit for philanthropy in providing these overalls. On economical grounds, which are the only grounds on which any expenditure of this sort is justified, the Corporation do what they can to make their own servants an example to the community in respect of clean habits. Could anything be more consonant with common-sense? There can be no doubt that our street-sweepers and dustmen daily carry to their homes quantities of dirt and filth which are caught by their clothes in the performance of their unpleasant work. These clothes they wear, day in day out, often for weeks without being washed. The dirt that is carried home is itself a source of mischief. Dirt makes dirt, and nowhere is it more likely to do so than in such homes as those of our poorer labourers. The Berlin scavenger divests himself of his canvas overalls whenever he reaches home—he may for the matter of that leave them behind the door—his ordinary clothes are not soiled and smeared with the dirt of his labour. He washes his hands, face, and neck, and is at once in a condition to enjoy his fireside— which he does not tarnish—or to take his wife and children out to some neighbouring park or garden to regale them and himself in the fresh air.

DOMESTIC SANITATION—MEAT INSPECTION

CHAPTER IV.

DOMESTIC SANITATION—MEAT INSPECTION.

Dwellings of the poor—Municipal energy—No slums in Berlin—Filthy dwellings not permitted—Treatment of dirty inhabitants—Shelters for the houseless—Persistent offenders against sanitation punished—Concurrence of inhabitants—Disinfection establishment—City cattle-market—City slaughter-house—Regulations for reception of cattle and dead meat—Meat inspection—Cattle-market, slaughtering, and inspection in one establishment—Inspecting staff—Veterinary surgeons—Female microscopists—Official guarantee for sound meat.

CONCERN for the public health (*Oeffentliche Gesundheit*) may now be said to dominate the mind of the Corporation; for, though a genuine and exemplary thoroughness characterises every part of their work, there is no department in which such salutary reforms have been effected as in that charged with the care of the health of the inhabitants. Whatever other reforms in administration may be minimised or postponed, any proposal that makes for the better sanitary condition of the people is sure to receive favourable consideration in the municipal council, and, if found practicable, is approved and carried out with a completeness which is only limited by a reasonable regard to economy. Mention has been made of the clearing out of the cellar dwellings, but this will hardly prepare those who know something of the squalor and misery prevailing in the slums of London, Liverpool, Glasgow, and in the lower quarters of our "own romantic town," to learn that there are no slums in Berlin. Yet this is the simple fact. Poverty there is; misery and suffering of the innocent by the ill-doing of others are common enough, as they are wherever frail human beings are gathered together; but filth, which is so usually the concomitant of poverty and crime, has no local habitation. For the past twenty years the Corporation have waged constant and successful war against dirt and material pollution among people and dwellings in any form in which these evils menace the general health of the community.

Every house proprietor is bound, when he finds his tenants keeping their dwellings in a filthy state, to warn them to cleanse them forthwith. If they do not, they are turned out without further ceremony. Should the landlord neglect or fail to perform his duty in this respect, a complaint made by the neighbours—a halfpenny post-card addressed to the proper quarter—will ensure a visit from an officer of the Sanitary Department. This officer will, if he finds the house filthy, order out the inhabitants, and cleanse it at the landlord's expense. "But do you not think you interfere too much with the liberty of the subject?" was the natural question. "Liberty of the subject? mein Herr," retorted Stadtrath Meubrink, to whom my best acknowledgments for most courteous attention are due; "Liberty of the subject? May I ask whether your theory of government is not the greatest happiness of the greatest number?" The reply was in the affirmative. "And have you not power to remove people from their houses when these become dangerous to the health of their neighbours?" "We have, when infectious disease breaks out among them." "Ah, but we anticipate you. We know that this dirt will gender and foster fever. We don't care to wait till fever breaks out. It may come in spite of us, through water or milk or otherwise; but we regard all fevers as preventable diseases, and we feel bound in the interest of the community to prevent them where we can. We too respect the liberty of the subject; but we deny the liberty of the subject to make himself or his home a source of danger to the health and life of his neighbours. We are just a little in advance of you in this matter."

There was no rational answer to this retort. There might have been, if it had been the case in Berlin that people, when thus turned out of house and home, were left to drift about the city in shelterless misery. But this is not so. It is far from the Berlin Corporation's idea of public economy that it should be so. Whenever these people are turned out — they are usually, of course, among the very poorest — the house is cleansed and purified, and the inmates are taken to Shelters (*Städtische Obdächer*) situated in different quarters of the city, and under the charge of the Poor Department. In these shelters they and their clothes are scrubbed and made clean. The workers among them are allowed to go out to their daily avocations, and daily they are made to cleanse themselves. Food is provided for them and their families at moderate cost, which is paid out of their earnings. If they are out of employment, they are put to some simple work within the shelter, and are paid for the work they perform. Persistent disregard of the rules of the shelter is treated as a police offence. After a few weeks' residence the people find themselves actually in some degree out of sympathy with uncleanly habits. They are then allowed once more to betake themselves to a home of their own, all the better for the lessons they have learned. This treatment is repeated where needful. But, when people remain incorrigibly dirty, their offence becomes a matter for the interference of the criminal authorities (*Polizei Behörde*). They are then drafted off to the sewage-fields or some other department of public work, where their earnings are used, in the first instance, to defray the cost of their own keep, the balance being applied in the next place to the maintenance of their families, who pass under the care of the authorities.

And this is all done with the assent and approval of the general population. German Socialism has its home and centre in the capital. Berlin is also the centre of German industry. Its population is for the most part a working-class population. The official, the wealthy, the artistic, the military, and the shopkeeping classes form in all but a small percentage of the whole. Yet, though in their meetings Socialists, and working men who are not Socialists, air their ideas and grievances, and declaim against the wealthy and the *bourgeoisie*, they have no quarrel with the treatment of those whose habits make them obnoxious to the public health. You may go through the quarters of the city where the very poorest live—you shall see many signs of poverty, scanty furnishings in the houses, poorly clad men and women, children running barefoot and bareheaded—yet they are clean, and for the most part even tidy. You shall see all this, but you shall find nothing corresponding to the filth and squalid wretchedness which meet you any hour of the day or night in the uncomely parts of our own city.

In 1886 the Corporation took another step in the interest of the public health by the erection of the first disinfection establishment (*Desinfectionsanstalt*) in Berlin. In every case where fever or infectious disease of any kind has been in a dwelling, the bed occupied by the patient, the clothing, linen, hangings, carpets, and other paraphernalia in any way likely to harbour germs of disease, are placed on a conveyance provided for the purpose, and carried off to this establishment. The waggon with its load is wheeled bodily into one of the apartments provided. The apartment is closed in, steam is passed through coil-pipes which encircle the room, till a temperature of 100° Celsius, or the boiling-point of water, is reached. For a period of thirty-five minutes the load is subjected to this heat, so that every germ is destroyed. Steam is then turned off, the apartment is reopened, and after the articles are cooled and ventilated they are sent home again purified and without damage. A small charge—three-halfpence per cubic mètre—is made on all goods disinfected in this manner. The establishment, which is centrally situated, occupies an area having a frontage of 142 and a depth of 120 feet. It is strongly built of brick and stone, while the rooms for the reception of articles to be disinfected are lined with iron, and can be hermetically closed. Infected goods are brought in by a gateway at one side of the building, and placed in a courtyard on what may be called the infected side, and in their turn are passed through the process of disinfection. Drawn out into a courtyard on the disinfected side, the purified articles are despatched by a separate gateway. All classes of the population are bound, in case of infectious disease visiting their homes, to use this means of purification. It has proved so beneficial and so acceptable to the community that it is now regarded as an indispensable adjunct to the administration of the Public Health Department.

The excitement which arose in Edinburgh last January on the question of diseased meat must still be fresh in the recollection of the citizens. Remembering the proposals then made in various quarters for transferring our slaughter-houses outside the city, establishing clearance-houses for dead meat, and the institution of a more efficient system of inspection, one turned with interest to inquire into the Berlin methods of dealing with the meat question. Here, again, the same characteristic energy was found going to the root of the matter and producing results which might stir the envy of even the best-governed municipalities in Britain. In 1864, Professor Virchow, moved by an alarming outbreak of trichinosis, warned the Corporation that the time had come for the erection of a communal slaughter-house and cattle-market, in which an efficient inspection could be maintained. Political troubles and the wars of 1866 and 1870 prevented the carrying out of these recommendations, with which the Town Council fully sympathised. Objections raised by the cattle trade and butchers, and even by sections of the public, had also to be overcome. But in the main public feeling, not only in Berlin but in other large towns in Germany, ran strongly in favour of the local authorities taking up the whole question of the killing and sale of meat intended for human food. In 1878 it was decided to erect a combined cattle-market and slaughter-house for the whole city. The site chosen was to the north-east of the town, convenient to the city railway, by which it could be brought into communication with all parts of the metropolis. As the city railway also communicates with the main lines, the transmission of cattle and of dead meat to and from the site could be accomplished with facility. In 1881 the undertaking was completed and opened for public use. An idea of the extent of the area occupied may be obtained when it is stated that fully 27 acres are covered by buildings. The watering of the vast establishment is accomplished by about sixteen miles of piping, while 3000 gas-jets are used for its illumination by night. The ground is covered with cement, which is easily and rapidly cleaned; and the fullest attention has been given to the perfect drainage of the place. All cattle to be offered for sale in the city of Berlin must be brought hither, and the slaughtering of cattle anywhere else within the municipal boundary is absolutely forbidden. For the reception of oxen, sheep, swine, and calves, different sheds are provided. Strict attention is given to the foddering and cleaning of the animals, and to the free ventilation of the stalls. On market-days all beasts sold for slaughter are transferred from the stalls of the dealers to the butchers' stalls, which are contiguous to the shambles. There is an immense open market for cattle, in which as many as 3800 animals at a time can be dealt with. In the open market for sheep and swine there is room enough to handle at one time 2500 and 8000 head respectively; whilst the trade in calves, which are bought and sold in large numbers, has likewise ample space assigned to it.

In the slaughtering department, what impresses the visitor most is the scrupulous cleanliness of the shambles not in immediate use, and the care that is taken to handle and dress the slaughtered meat with the utmost promptitude and despatch. This is the more necessary in the case of meat destined for the country and for other cities; for it should be remembered that meat is slaughtered in Berlin for consumption in distant towns, and even in Paris itself. For the benefit of the large Jewish population, special arrangements are made for the slaughtering of animals according to Jewish rites. The apartments in which the manufacture of albumen, condensing of blood, dressing of tripe, and cleansing of skins are carried on, are models of cleanliness and good order. In the slaughter-house proper, over and above the accommodation already mentioned, three cattle-stalls accommodate 1300 head; there are four swine-stalls holding 3400, and stalls accommodating 2000 sheep and as many calves. The ordinary staff of the establishment is quite able to overtake the slaughtering and dressing of all these animals in one day. The total cost of the combined establishment reached almost half a million sterling, of which £300,000 may be set down to the cattle-market, and £200,000 to the slaughter-house. As many as 1,100,000 head are slaughtered annually. After liberal grants towards redemption of capital and all charges for maintenance, the establishment yields an annual revenue equal to fully four per cent on the original cost.

Not only are the cattle-market and slaughter-houses combined in this central institution, but here also is set up what is probably the most efficient system of meat inspection in the world. All dead meat slaughtered in the country or abroad, and intended for Berlin consumption, must be brought here for inspection before being offered for sale as human food. No butcher in Berlin may offer meat for human consumption which does not bear the official stamp of the inspecting department of the central market. Under the chief inspector of meat, who is a veterinary surgeon of high qualification, there are at present no fewer than twenty-two surgeons and assistant-surgeons, with a large staff of special inspectors, microscopists, and stampers. Belonging to the staff there are forty-five women trained to the use of the microscope. Their business is to examine and report upon specimens of tissue or blood brought from the inspection houses, where the surgeons are engaged examining carcasses slaughtered on the premises or brought from a distance. On completing their reports, the microscopists pass them on to the surgeon in charge of their room, and he in turn reports to his chief, who condemns whatever meat is proved to be unsound. These women work but five hours a-day, as the constant use of the microscope severely strains the eyes. They have each a salary of about £75 per annum. So thorough is the inspection—and the thoroughness is secured by the number and competency of the staff—that it is all but impossible for a diseased carcass to pass out of the market. The result is that one may enter any butcher's shop in Berlin and be sure that all the fresh meat there offered for sale has undergone a strict scientific test, and has been officially declared fit for human food. It should be kept in mind that the whole cost of inspection is part of the general expenses of the market, and has been defrayed before the profits above shown are brought out. All meat that has been condemned as unsound is not necessarily destroyed. Carcasses of animals which have suffered from tubercle, trichinosis, anthrax, and other dangerous diseases are, of course, destroyed. But carcasses showing only local unsoundness, and carcasses known in this country as "braxy," are treated by what is known as Rohrbeck's process of disinfection, and are then found perfectly safe for human food, and as nourishing as ordinarily healthy meat. This class of meat is permitted to be sold in shops set apart for the purpose. It is ticketed, so that purchasers know what they are buying. As it is much cheaper than other meat, it is largely used by the poorer classes. In warm weather special arrangements are made for keeping all the meat at a low temperature till it is delivered to the shops for sale, and the utmost speed is shown in passing the carcass through the necessary processes, including that of inspection. Thus complaints about meat getting deteriorated through delay and handling are seldom heard. The whole cattle and butcher trades of Berlin appear to be so satisfied with the working of the present system that they would on no account return to the old state of things.

PUBLIC HOSPITALS—CONVALESCENT HOMES

CHAPTER V.

PUBLIC HOSPITALS AND CONVALESCENT HOMES.

Municipal control of public hospitals — Private hospitals — Treatment of infectious disease — The Moabit Hospital — Its structure and administration — Its drainage — Friedrichshain Hospital — Urban Hospital — Pavilion system — General equipment — Paying patients — Cost of maintenance in different hospitals — Detailed accounts and statistics — Nursing — Victoria Training Institution — Convalescent homes — How justified — Lymph Institute of Berlin — Public baths.

IN connection with the subject of public health, the municipal hospital system of Berlin is worthy of special study. Among Continental medical schools, Berlin ranks with Paris and Vienna; while some of her physicians and surgeons—Virchow, Waldeyer, Martin, Koch, and Von Bergmann—stand pre-eminent among the most famous doctors of the present day. The relation of the city hospitals to the Medical School of

Berlin is now one of great practical importance; but for the present purpose these valuable institutions can only be considered in their more public and general relation to the municipality.

It has already been remarked that in all establishments in whose administration the Corporation take part, the same efficient and vigorous management which obtains in the purely civic departments is found to prevail. Whenever the town takes up their administration, then they are managed as municipal concerns—their income is municipal income, their expenditure is municipal expenditure—their whole affairs are published in the municipal reports, and are as open to public scrutiny as the cleaning or lighting of the thoroughfares. It is so with the administration of the public schools, orphan homes, asylums, and workhouses. It is so with the public infirmaries. As in other cities, there are in Berlin many institutions for the relief of the sick and infirm, which have been founded, some of them centuries ago, by private benefaction, and which are maintained partly by the charity of individuals and partly by payments made by the inmates themselves. In Berlin, also, some eminent doctors keep hospitals for the treatment of cases falling under their own specialty, and for clinical instruction to their own students. The town is not asked to bear any part of the cost of such institutions, and it takes nothing to do with their management. But the principal infirmaries are under the direct control of the Corporation. The largest hospital in the city, the Charité, was the great public infirmary of Berlin prior to 1872. It used to be conducted on the lines which Edinburgh medical students of the last generation will remember in connection with the old Royal Infirmary. It received all classes of ailments—infectious, contagious, and ordinary; and not infrequently, within comparatively recent times, there have occurred within its walls outbreaks of secondary infection which greatly bewildered the medical staff, but which admit of very simple explanation with our present-day knowledge.

In the matter of the treatment of infectious disease, Berlin was indeed no better off twenty years ago than some towns nearer home; albeit when infectious disease did break out, its low sanitary condition afforded a too congenial soil for the spread of the invasion. Cholera and smallpox always found a happy hunting-ground in Berlin, until what may be called its municipal renascence in 1872. Invasions of these diseases had been met by the erection of wooden sheds in open spaces, with such temporary devices for disinfection and purification as the circumstances might suggest. The spaces were cleared, and the whole *débris* of the erections was consumed so soon as the calamity was over. One large space had always been reserved by the Corporation in the Moabit district from the time of the cholera epidemic in 1832; and here, as occasion arose, the largest receptacles were erected for the reception of sufferers from different plagues. During the war of 1870-71, when large numbers of French prisoners were interned in the city, smallpox broke out among them with great virulence. Erections were again run up at Moabit, and after a prolonged struggle the disease was finally subdued. By this time, however, the labours and exhortations of Virchow and others were winning over members of the Corporation to a true sense of what the public health required. Virchow, from his place in the Town Council, did not fail to press home the lessons taught by repeated visitations of disease which proper sanitary precautions might have prevented or largely mitigated. The Corporation resolved that the old methods of meeting such outbreaks must be abandoned, and that buildings should be erected and kept in a state of permanent preparation for the reception and treatment of epidemic victims. This resolution was no sooner passed than the erection of a set of sixteen wards on the site of the old barracks at Moabit was put in hand. These were built in framework of wood and brick. In three months the sixteen, with all furnishings and proper adjuncts, were completed at a cost of £30,000. Subsequent extensions have taken place, and the Moabit Hospital is now one of the largest and best appointed in Germany. It comprises in all thirty wards, ranged on two sides of an extended parallelogram. They are separated from each other by a space of 56 feet, while there is an intervening grass-covered space of 200 feet width between the sides of the parallelogram. There are thirty beds in each ward, so that the hospital can accommodate at least 900 patients. The administration buildings, as well as the kitchen, laundry, and other offices, stand in separate structures. Each ward is entered by a corridor, on either side of which are lavatory and bathing accommodation, a tea kitchen for the preparation of small refections, and day-rooms for the nurses. The walls are of strong framework and oil-painted within, so that they can be easily washed. The outside is covered with fireproof felting. The walls stand fully 10 feet high, the roof and ceiling are sloped, and the height from the centre of the floor to the ceiling ventilators is 15 feet. Abundance of light is afforded by means of twenty-eight windows in each ward, or nearly a window to each bed. The roof is so fitted with a system of ventilating valves that a constant supply of pure air is preserved in the apartment; and there is an even temperature maintained by a complete heating apparatus. In this hospital, as in the Friedrichshain and the recently erected Urban, there is a disinfection house, which is used not only for articles belonging to the hospital, but also for the clothes and other property of the patients. In each hospital also there are special observation wards, completely isolated, where doubtful cases are placed until the true nature of the illness is ascertained. Although at first intended only for infectious ailments, the Moabit has come to be used as a general hospital. Indeed there is no hospital exclusively devoted to febrile disease. It is, however, still to the Moabit that the greater number of infectious cases are taken, and such diseases as cholera and smallpox would be exclusively treated there, unless an epidemic of unusual severity rendered additional erections necessary.[1] It has a separate drainage system of its own, which is well served with strong disinfectants. The system connects with the main sewage system at a distant point. This separate drainage accounts for the large water consumption at the Moabit. For the use of patients and for cooking purposes, the water daily supplied is about twenty-four gallons per head; but when

[1] The Moabit was kept in constant readiness for cases of cholera during the recent visitation.

the supply for flushing the drains, feeding the heating apparatus, and watering the grass plots and flower-beds is taken into account, the daily consumpt averages six times that quantity, or nearly 150 gallons per head. The Moabit Hospital has been described here mainly because it affords a fair example of how a perfectly satisfactory establishment may be constructed at a moderate cost, with the fullest regard to modern sanitary requirements, provided it is not thought necessary to use stone and lime. These framework sick-rooms appear thoroughly sound, and seem likely to last for an indefinite time. Yet the entire hospital, with all its equipment of offices, kitchens, engine-room, and heating apparatus, represents a cost of but little over £100 per bed.

Other two public hospitals, the Friedrichshain and Urban, deserve mention. Both were originated by bequests left to the charge of the Corporation by benevolent persons. The bequests were only intended as the nucleus of the total fund required, but looking to the extension of the city, the Corporation in each case adopted the donor's suggestion, and provided the remainder of the funds out of the town treasury. Friedrichshain was opened in 1874, the Urban only in 1890. In both of these hospitals the pavilion system has been adopted, each pavilion having two wards, one on the ground-floor and one above. Unlike the Moabit, they are substantially built in variegated brick and stone work, and have a solid and even stately appearance. Every improvement which modern knowledge and experience could suggest has been introduced in these hospitals. In the Urban there is a complete installation of the electric light. Each pavilion is devoted to a separate class of ailment, and is so independent of its neighbours that the risk of mischief from secondary infection is reduced to a minimum. An underground passage connects the pavilion with the engine-room and other service establishments, and also, it must be added, with the dissecting rooms and the mortuary. Adjoining the mortuary in each hospital there is a tastefully arranged little chapel entering directly from outside the premises, where friends of deceased patients may attend funeral services, and pass out again without requiring to go through the building or grounds. Any one who would see the perfection of hospital equipment, in which the most scientific ideas of modern requirements are generously and faithfully applied, should see the Urban in Berlin. It contains accommodation for 600 patients, and the whole establishment, with its furnishings and plenishings complete, was opened at a cost of only £245 per bed.

It may be interesting to note the cost of patients in the leading hospitals, keeping in mind that the treatment in all accords with the best sanctions of medical skill, and that the food is at least as good as a well-to-do working man would be thoroughly pleased with. In the Charité, the daily cost is one and a half mark per head, or £27, 10s. a-year; in the Moabit it is 2.7858, or £50, 10s. a-year; in the Friedrichshain 3.076, or £56 a-year; and in the Urban 3.975, or £72 a-year. If patients can afford it out of their own means, or through friendly or sick societies with which they may be connected, they are expected to pay something towards their maintenance; and it is not uncommon to find patients cheerfully paying the whole cost of their board and lodging. In the Friedrichshain and Urban there are small private wards, in which patients who can afford a higher than the ordinary rate of board may be accommodated. To the Charité are sent the greater proportion of patients who contribute nothing to their own maintenance, and for these the town pays to the hospital funds at the rate of 12s. 3d. per week for adults, and 8s. 9d. for children under 12. Including the Charité, the principal public hospitals provide accommodation for over 3000 invalids. All receipts from patients are duly credited to the respective hospital accounts, and go to diminish the annual expenditure, the balance of which is carried to the debit of the city accounts. In none of the hospitals is there any sign of stint or parsimony; but nothing is allowed to go to waste. In the accounts of the Urban you shall find even the proceeds of old shoes duly accounted for under the head of miscellaneous receipts. Next to seeing the hospital itself, the best thing one interested in the subject can do is to study the elaborate reports issued yearly in the municipal Brown-book. In these reports one finds most instructive details of the whole work in each of the public hospitals. Not only are the capital and revenue accounts set forth with clearness and amplitude, but the cases are classified according to the ailments treated. Where surgical interference has become necessary, the kind of operation performed in each case is specified, and all results, whether of medical or surgical treatment, are carefully tabulated. These reports will, in course of a few years, prove invaluable to medical registrars and statisticians throughout the world. Perhaps it is worth noting, as a word to the wise, that, while the positions of house physicians and surgeons in these hospitals are coveted by the best students, the Corporation assign a salary of from £50 to £75 per annum, besides free board and lodging, to such appointments. The principal medical officers — who may also be private consultants—receive £300 to £350 per annum. After deducting the income from patients and interest on foundation bequests, the net daily cost to the city per patient is, in the Moabit Hospital, 2.0613 marks, or £38, 4s. per annum; in the Friedrichshain 2.005, or £36, 10s. per annum; and in the Urban 3.155, or £57, 10s. per annum. The total net expenditure in connection with the three hospitals is estimated for the current year at nearly £60,000, and this will be wholly borne by the ratepayers of Berlin.

The art of nursing has been developed quite as successfully in Berlin as among ourselves. In all the principal hospitals trained nurses are employed. Many of them are ladies who have devoted themselves to this work from motives of benevolence; all are women of good education, who have taken, or are about to take, certificates in prescribed courses of training. A staff nurse usually has charge of from twenty to thirty-five patients, and she is supported by one, or, more frequently, two assistants. In some of the hospitals duly qualified male nurses are employed, but they are a small minority. In the leading hospitals—the Friedrichshain and the Urban—special training schools for nurses have been established, and the fees paid by the probationers form part of the hospital revenue. These schools are carried on in connection with the Victoria Training Institution for Nurses, which was started under the auspices of the Empress Frederick when she was Imperial Crown Princess, and which bears her name. From this institution nurses are now sent all over Germany.

Any description of the hospital system of Berlin must be inadequate without a single reference to the treatment of convalescent patients. Upon the principle that what is worth doing is worth doing well, the Corporation resolved that the cure of patients under their care should be complete. It was found that large numbers of patients passing through the hospitals were obliged to return to work before their strength was completely restored, and that in consequence many broke down and became a burden on the Commission for the Poor—that is, they became chargeable to the rates. Accordingly, convalescent homes have been established on the various drainage estates belonging to the city, where patients, unable to procure for themselves needful rest and nourishment after a time of severe illness, are maintained for two or three weeks before being allowed to resume work. Members of the Corporation, in showing visitors over these homes, are careful to explain that they are kept up not from feelings of charity, but from the purest economical considerations. They justify the cost of the homes on the ground that it is, in the long-run, less of a burden on the community than would be the cost of maintaining many of those patients and their families if, for want of proper treatment during convalescence, they were to become so enfeebled as to be unable to provide for themselves and those dependent on them.

Under the Public Health Department there is an establishment within the slaughter-houses for the collection and preparation of lymph for vaccination purposes. Sound healthy calves are inoculated, and pure lymph is collected from them. The fluid is then carefully treated under strict scientific supervision. It is put up in small phials, hermetically sealed, and distributed for medical use all over the empire. So famous, indeed, has the Berlin lymph become, that large quantities are now exported to Great Britain and America, where medical men prefer it to any other kind.

Zealous regard for the public health is also shown in the number of municipal bathing-places which now exist. There are at the present time no fewer than twelve public bathing-establishments, with swimming-baths attached, in different parts of the city, and three others on a much enlarged scale have been projected. They are largely patronised by the working-class population, male and female, and are becoming more popular every year. Very moderate charges are made for admission; and every inducement is given, by way of swimming *fêtes* and competitions, to encourage the public to take full advantage of this means of healthful and cleanly recreation.

ADMINISTRATION FOR RELIEF OF THE POOR

CHAPTER VI.

ADMINISTRATION FOR RELIEF OF THE POOR.

Old methods of relief—Scheme of the Great Elector—Public obligation for the poor recognised in 1820—Single Poor Board for Berlin—District committees—Unpaid inspection—Outdoor relief—Discrimination in relief—District physicians and surgeons—Workhouses—Incorrigible poor—Habitual offenders—Night refuges and shelters—Care of poor children—Old married couples—Orphan poor—Orphan depot—Boarding out—Education of out-boarders—Sick poor—Dalldorf Institution for Imbeciles—Union for Prevention of Pauperisation—Its methods and success—Comparative cost of Berlin poor administration.

Down to the time of the Great Elector no serious effort had ever been made to systematise the treatment of the poor. But that Prince, while occupied in extending the power and influence of Prussia abroad, had a keen desire for reform at home. Offended by the prevalence of street-begging in Berlin, he called upon the town authorities to prepare for his consideration a scheme by which some provision should be made for the helpless and deserving poor. But the town authorities of those days were quite unequal to such a task. They could offer no other counsel than that the beggars should be allowed to seek alms from door to door instead of on the public streets, and that only those should be permitted to beg who were certified by the authorities, the sign of which should be a pewter badge worn on the coat. They were to wander from door to door like so many Edie Ochiltrees, with right to refer to their pewter badges in token of their licence. " It is little we can do, your Electoral Highness, having neither the means nor the *nervus rerum gerundarum* wherewith to help the poor and abolish public begging. We see many needy people reduced in the world who are in far greater want than those who will come for badges, but who, on account of their former circumstances, are ashamed to beg. They prefer to die; and as for us, we hardly know how to provide coffins to bury them. It were, indeed, a great boon to have some sort of weekly pittance secured to such people, but we can't find it. Would not your Electoral Highness graciously open the electoral purse somewhat and assist in the business?" Whether the municipal worthies of that day occupied themselves too much with politics or with personal squabbles, they proved themselves, in the opinion of his Highness, quite incompetent to deal with questions affecting the poor. The result of much feeble reporting and discussion was that Frederick took the whole affair into his own hands, and established an Electoral Commission (*Kurfürstliche Kommission wegen des Armenwesens*), which afterwards became a Royal Direction of the Poor in Berlin. The funds at the disposal of the Direction were raised partly by an annual grant from the royal purse, and partly by contributions from the benevolent, and from church-door collections, for which special appeals were made in the royal name from time to time. This form of paternal administration continued down to 1820, when the public obligation to provide for the poor came to be more fully recognised, and the charge of the poor who received outdoor relief, and of the almshouses, which, mainly through private charity, had been founded under the Direction, passed into the hands of the Corporation. The great increase of the city since 1820 has made it imperative that the poor department, like all other parts of the municipal administration, should receive more adequate handling. In 1853 it was resolved by the Corporation to deal with the whole question in a manner commensurate with the largely increased necessities of the case. The resolution took many years, however, to develop; and indeed it was not till 1886 that the now admirably organised system received its finishing touches.

There is only one administration for the poor in Berlin (*die Städtische Armenpflege*). It embraces the care of the homeless poor, the relief of the necessitous who have homes of their own, the care of orphans, the treatment of incurables, of imbeciles, and of the insane. It also extends to the assistance of persons in temporary distress by means of redeemable grants, to night asylums for the houseless, and to the correction of habitual offenders and persons under the supervision of the police. Besides the Town Council, the department embraces no fewer than 2259 burghers, chosen from the municipal divisions of the city with special reference to their knowledge of their own localities. For the purpose of the relief of the poor the city is divided into 234 separate districts. In each district there is a committee of from four to twelve members, whose chairman is usually the councillor of the ward in which the district is situated. These committees make careful inquiry into each case as it comes before them for relief, and by frequent visits among the poor—as in the case of our own Destitute Sick Society—the members satisfy themselves how far relief should be granted, continued, or withdrawn. Such visits are not left to paid officials of the department, and in this way there is an agreeable absence of the bumbledom that often discredits our poor administration at home. The department also provides about seventy-five physicians and surgeons, who visit the poor in their own homes, and to whom an annual allowance of from £60 to £90 is paid. Careful discrimination is made between the innocently poor and those whose poverty is the direct consequence of their own misdeeds. Of 19,610 adults who received outdoor relief in 1891, more than 56 per cent. were over 65 years of age, more than 30 per cent. suffered from chronic ailments or were incurable, and over 12 per cent. were able to earn only part of the necessaries of life. In the same year there were 8024 children receiving outdoor relief, besides 5156 poor orphans maintained in the orphan homes or boarded out in families. Among the total of 27,634 persons receiving outdoor relief, there was distributed, including extra assistance in particular cases, the sum of 3,736,692 marks, equal to about £180,000 sterling. Of the adults receiving relief nearly three-fourths were women.

While the greater part of the funds raised from the rates for the relief of the poor is distributed in outdoor relief under the direction of the district committees, there are almshouses for the reception of the poor who are no longer able to keep a house over their head, and there are workhouses for those who cannot be trusted with money grants. No person receives outdoor relief who does not bear a respectable character. At Rummelsburg, one of the large sewage estates, the principal workhouse has been established. It contains about 1800 inmates, of whom 1430 are poor through their own fault, and almost all are police offenders. The remainder are subjects of chronic illness, in most cases the result of their own vicious habits of life. The latter class live apart in the hospital section of the establishment, where they receive medical treatment. The two classes are named respectively the *Korrigenden* and the *Hospitaliten*— that is to say, the first class consists of persons who have either actually been, or were in danger of becoming, the subjects of police correction the latter are invalids, for the most part worn out and helpless. In so far as they are able-bodied, the first class are put to work on the fields in the neighbourhood of the workhouse, and are treated as if they might yet become respectable members of society. They are kept to steady employment, get sound plain food, are obliged to lead a regular life, and when it appears that they are safe to be trusted once more to maintain themselves in an honourable way, they are permitted to return to whatever decent employment they can obtain. Many men and not a few women are thus detained in the workhouse for years, not because they cannot work, but because they have not moral stamina enough to prevent them from becoming pests to the community if they were at large. In short, at Rummelsburg you shall see fully at work the Berliners' method of treating their police-court criminals, their habitual drunkards, wife-beaters, and street-brawlers. Such persons are not allowed to go at large after enduring the short term of imprisonment which is the immediate punishment of their offences. They are looked upon as hinderers of decent industry, and as likely to make other people like themselves if they are left at liberty. If permitted to drift about they would only be a source of mischief and would sorn on the community. The community simply refuses to be sorned upon by them, and packs them off to Rummelsburg, where they may have a chance of mending their ways, and where they are meanwhile compelled to do at least some work for the bread they eat. All such persons are subject to a longer or shorter period of police supervision; and it is, after all, a merciful arrangement that during that period they should be under such reformatory treatment as may perchance result in their ultimate restoration to respectable life.

Under the poor administration there are also night asylums for wanderers, as well as the shelters for the homeless, of which mention has been previously made. The only remark that is required about them is that full inquiry is made into the circumstances of each case, and, as far as possible, assistance and further shelter are afforded to those who are found able and anxious to work.

If the municipality is strict and rigid with its vicious poor, it is tender in its treatment of the respectable aged and of orphans. With us the principle of poor administration is to make all relief from the rates as disagreeable as possible to those who receive it, whether their poverty is due to their own fault or not. It is not so in

Berlin. In the case of old married couples, for example, there is a benevolent provision by which, if it can be shown that they have led honourable lives, and are not responsible for their own misfortunes, they are not separated from each other on being received into the almshouses. The late Emperor William celebrated his golden wedding in 1879 by founding a Home for the reception of such couples, and named it after himself and the Empress Augusta (*Die Alterversorgungsanstalt der Kaiser Wilhelm und Augusta-Stiftung*).

In their care of the orphan poor the administration do not visit the iniquities of the fathers upon the children. In the centre of the city there is an Orphan Depot (*Waisen-Depot*) where children are received and housed for a time until full inquiry can be made into their antecedents, state of health, mental abilities, and natural disposition. Thereafter they are either transferred to the Orphan House at Rummelsburg, or are boarded out. There are over 5000 orphans under the charge of the municipality, and of these more than four-fifths are boarded out in families which have been carefully selected by the district committees. The children are sent to the common schools of the town, where they mingle with the children of ordinary citizens, and as far as possible any stigma attaching to the fact that they are maintained at the public cost is sought to be removed. After leaving school they are put to various occupations—the boys to handicrafts and the girls for the most part to domestic service. Their future career is carefully watched until they grow up to maturity. If it be true that only two per cent of the Berliners go to church, it must be granted that they give much attention to the moral and religious training of these poor children. All of them, before they pass out of the care of the department, are, if they are Protestants, confirmed in the Reformed Church, and if they are Catholics, are sent for confirmation by a Catholic bishop. It is claimed by the administration, from the reports which they annually receive of the conduct of the children after they have begun life for themselves, that these orphans turn out, on the whole, better than other children, and that of the girls 98 per cent. do well. The city charges itself also with the cost of the hospital treatment of all the sick, incurable, and insane who are unable to pay for themselves, even though they may not otherwise be indebted to public charity. The Charité Hospital receives the greater number of the administration's patients, but other hospitals are used in the case of sufferers from special disorders, such as diseases of the skin, eye, throat, and so forth. By a royal grant, the town is entitled to place in the Charité every year, free of charge, as many patients as would together represent 100,000 hospital days of a single patient. For the remainder, in the Charité and in the other hospitals, the usual charge against the Poor Administration for adult patients is 1.75 mark, and for children under twelve years of age, 1.25 mark per day. For insane patients the administration pay as much as 3 marks per day.

The excellent institution for imbeciles and idiots belonging to the city at Dalldorf, where over 1200 men, women, and children are maintained, is worthy of particular description; but it must suffice here to mention that in the completeness of its appointments and sanitary arrangements, as well as in its architectural appearance, it is equal to any of the recently constructed public institutions; and that the cost to the town, including all the working expenses of the establishment, is under 2 marks per patient per day.

One important form of relief has been for some years in existence which is worthy of special notice. It was recognised that many excellent people occasionally fall into distress through innocent misfortune, who yet, for obvious reasons, are not suitable objects for relief from the rates, but rather deserve, if possible, to be saved from accepting such a form of charity. Accordingly, in the year 1869, there was established a Union for the Prevention of Pauperisation (*Verein gegen Verarmung*), having for its object the relief of industrious persons in temporary distress. The idea took hold of the public mind, and the funds of the Union have been augmented from year to year by large gifts and bequests, until now they amount to a capital sum of about £700,000. From the yearly revenue of the Union, assistance in various forms, sometimes to the amount of £30 in a year, is afforded to persons who are found eligible. During a period of sixteen years there have been given out of this fund donations to the extent of 888,020 marks, distributed among 56,188 persons. There have also been given among 15,288 persons, by way of loans, repayable on their circumstances improving, sums amounting to 851,875 marks. Of the latter amount, 568,811 marks have been repaid to the fund—a pleasing testimony to the worthiness of those who were aided. Moreover, as many as 3258 sewing-machines have, during the same period, been gifted or loaned to needle-women. In dealing with persons receiving assistance in this way, great care is taken to avoid impairing their self-respect, and to encourage them to renewed industry in order to regain a position of independence. This fund is rapidly gaining the confidence of those who wish to help people who are willing to help themselves. During the past five years it has been enriched, through legacies and donations, to the extent of a million of marks per annum. It has been said on good authority that the magistrates of Edinburgh need never want the means of giving judicious aid to victims of innocent distress, so willing are many to give to such an object if only the proper means could be devised for rendering assistance to the right people. It will be worth while, if an attempt should be made to organise such a form of benefaction in Edinburgh or elsewhere, to inquire fully into the details of the administration of the Berlin Union against Pauperisation.

A competent authority has stated that in Edinburgh there is expended annually in public charity, including poor-rates and hospital subscriptions, as much as £250,000. This would mean that Berlin, giving to these objects in the same proportion, should expend annually not less than a million and a half. In point of fact, however, the estimates for the current year show that Berlin will spend upon all the objects which have been described in this chapter, with the exception of the Union Fund, and upon the city hospitals and convalescent homes, not more than £542,000, or about one-third in proportion to our expenditure; and it is doubtful whether any town in Britain is able to show as good value for its money.

EDUCATION AND THE COMMON SCHOOLS

CHAPTER VII.

EDUCATION AND THE COMMON SCHOOLS.

Civic control of all schools — School Deputation — Management of the common schools — School Commission — Inspectors — Statistics of school-going population — Classes in common schools — School age — Subjects taught — Examinations — School hours — Holidays — Music and gymnastics — Manners — Treatment of irregular attendance — Religious instruction — Punishments — Natural history excursions — Museum instruction — Continuation schools — Trade schools — Schools for the blind and deaf mutes — Annual cost of department.

THE administration of the town schools, common and upper, is vested in a deputation (*Städtische Schul-Deputation*), which has its headquarters in the council chambers, and is composed of magistrates, town councillors, and representatives of the school commissioners, about thirty members in all. This body has authority over the public schools and furnishings, resolves as to the erection of new schools, appoints teachers, deals with reports of the inspectors, and through the school commissioners (*Schul - Deputirten*) maintains regular visitation of the schools and inquiry into cases of discipline. It also has the oversight of private schools and private teachers. For the purpose of educational inspection the schools are grouped within sixteen districts, with a member of the deputation as superintendent of each. There are eight qualified professional inspectors of schools (*Schul - Inspectoren*) for the whole city, and each is charged with the regular educational inspection of all the schools in two of the districts, having the superintendent of the district as his immediate municipal superior. Each school, on the other hand, is under the charge of a committee (*Schul-Commission*), consisting chiefly of citizens who have been chosen by the electors as deputies (*Bürger-Deputirten*) to act as members of the general school administration. At present there are 150 school committees, with from ten to twelve members each. In some instances one committee may have charge of two or even three schools. The school is administered by the teaching staff, the visiting committee, the inspectors, and, over all, the School Deputation. Excluding the University, there are 385 separate educational establishments including common, higher, and private schools, and of these there are close on 190 common schools (*Gemeinde-Schulen*) corresponding to our board schools. Beyond making sure that the teachers are duly qualified, and that pupils passing from them into the universities are fully prepared, the municipality takes no control of the private schools, which number about eighty in all.

With the late Matthew Arnold's book on the Higher Schools and Universities of Germany open to all readers, it would be superfluous to enter here upon any description of the municipal higher schools of Berlin. These correspond in their scope and culture with those throughout Germany, whose work and management are prescribed by State regulations. In the higher schools for girls (*Höhere Mädchen-Schulen*) pupils are taught all the branches of a refined education. In the higher burger schools and the upper modern schools (*Höhere Bürger-Schulen* and *Obere*

Real-Schulen), boys are educated with a view to their fitness for general business and the higher departments of commercial life. In the gymnasial schools (*Gymnasien*), boys intended for a professional career are prepared for the universities, which are usually entered at the age of eighteen. But our chief concern at present is with the common schools. Of 228,000 pupils attending school this year, 175,000 are at the common schools, 33,000 at the higher schools, and 20,000 at private schools. The last mentioned schools are attended for the most part by children of the richest classes, and by children from other countries.

Fourteen per cent. of the population of Berlin are at school. This is about two per cent. more than in Edinburgh, which is probably the most school-going city in the United Kingdom. Education is compulsory. In the common schools it is free. In the higher schools the annual fees are from 80 to 100 marks, or £4 to £5 per pupil; and the third of every three members of a family attending school at the same time is usually a free pupil. Every child must begin to attend school at the age of six, and must continue till it reaches fourteen. By a recent change in the law, the practice of children within school age commencing work in factories, and giving three hours' daily attendance at school, has been disallowed. All, therefore, that a child is capable of learning in the subjects taught in the common schools up to the age of fourteen is now ensured to it before the labour for existence begins.

Each common school is divided into six classes, and each class has two divisions—a lower and a higher. Entering at the age of six, a child commences with the lower division of the sixth class, where the first half of the school year is spent. The upper division is passed through in the second half of the year. Before a child is allowed to pass into a higher class, or into the higher division of a class, it must be certified to be fit to do so. It may thus happen that a dull or stupid child will get no further than the third or fourth class by the time it reaches the age of fourteen, and is permitted to leave school to begin work. On the other hand, a child of good parts, which requires to spend only one year in each of the four lower classes, may spend two years in each of the two upper classes, and so obtain a thoroughly competent hold of the higher branches there taught. These six classes range from number six to number one. In the sixth class the child learns the elements of reading, and makes a simple beginning in writing, arithmetic, singing, drawing, and Bible knowledge. To these are added gymnastics in the fifth class. In the fourth class a beginning is made with geometry, physics, and natural history. In the third class the same subjects are developed, with the addition of Latin and ancient history. The second class finds the pupil busy with botany, French, mineralogy, and the history of the middle ages; while in the first class, English, modern history, the literature of his own country, algebra, physiology, and shorthand occupy his energies. Examinations are conducted with strict regard to the ground the pupil has been taken over in each subject; he therefore presents himself to the examiner without the labour and excitement of tumultuous cramming. Indeed cramming is relentlessly suppressed in Germany. Examinations take place twice a-year, at Easter and in October. At these examinations children are certified as ripe (*reif*) for advancement to higher grades, or as unripe (*unreij*), when they must remain where they are.

School begins at seven in the morning in summer and eight in winter; and it continues till eleven, with half an hour's interval from nine till half-past nine o'clock for breakfast and play. At eleven o'clock the scholars go home to dinner. They return at one and remain till four, when school is done for the day. But they take tasks home that occupy them several hours in the evening. The actual time devoted to lessons in school is six and a half hours per day. On Wednesdays and Saturdays there is no afternoon school, and the free hours are given chiefly to gymnastic exercises, which are diligently cultivated, and, in the upper classes, to botanising excursions or visits to industrial and other museums. The total number of hours per week devoted to lessons within school is thirty-three; the time given to gymnastics, botanising, and visiting museums, though more exhilarating, is also spent under the eye of the teacher, while the hours required for exercises at home make a heavy drain upon the scholar's strength. Only hardy children are found able to stand it all, and matters have become so grave that proposals are now under consideration by which the burden may be made less, and more time given for play and unrestrained relaxation. It is felt that these boons can be gained without really impairing the value or efficiency of the school-work, and it is already evident they will be speedily introduced. The school year begins at Easter. At Whitsuntide there is a week's holiday; in summer—July or August—four weeks; in October one week, at Christmas two weeks, and at Easter two weeks. The holidays thus extend to ten weeks in the year. In warm weather, when the thermometer any day shows 77 degs. Fahr. in the shade at 10 A.M., all the schools cease work at eleven o'clock for that day.

In the principal parks spaces are set apart, and gymnastic apparatus of all sorts provided for the use of the common school children under the guidance of their teachers. The prominence given to gymnastics and music—especially choral and part singing—relieves to some extent, it must be admitted, the too arduous nature of the school-work. The one develops a healthy body, the other clears and invigorates the mind. Music and song are zealously cultivated. Every German boy or girl who has left school can read music so as to be able to sing almost at sight. German soldiers enliven long marches in field manœuvres by singing in chorus. During the Franco-Prussian war they often marched into action singing the melodies and hymns of the Fatherland;[1] and when, as occasionally happens in Berlin, beer-drinking boozers are staggering home from a late carouse, they do not make night hideous with yells, but help each other along to the tune of some catch or glee.

Careful attention is always given to the manners of the children. Every boy takes off his cap to his teacher, and the rules of politeness are strictly insisted upon. The result is that even among the humblest labouring classes courtesy

---

[1] We know something of this ourselves; for I believe it is a well-authenticated fact that some of the Scottish regiments went under fire at Waterloo singing "Scots wha hae."

and civility are observed, and a stranger moving among the people is sensible of an addition to the amenities of life in observing the politeness of their behaviour.

Absence from school is severely dealt with. It is the duty of the school committee to order inquiry into every case of absence or of frequent lateness. If the child has left home and loitered, it has to suffer punishment; but if the parents are to blame in not getting the child ready in time, or are wilfully keeping it from school, they are fined after a second warning. Due allowance is always made when the parents can show good cause for the absence of the child.

During the whole of the school years two hours a-week are devoted to religious instruction; and for convenience in this respect several schools receive only Catholic children who are taught by teachers of their own faith. In thirty-five of the common schools provision is made for the religious instruction of Jewish children, by teachers of their own persuasion. It is part of the administrative regulations that all the children attending the common schools—except Jewish children — shall become connected with the Christian Church before the completion of their school years—that is, before the age of fourteen. Catholic and Protestant children are prepared for confirmation by their respective clergy; and it is the duty of the school authorities to see that every child has been confirmed before the leaving certificate is granted.

Faithful record is kept of each child's behaviour, as well as of its progress in knowledge; and the records are regularly inspected by the school committee. When bad behaviour is persistent the parents are called before the committee and invited to co-operate in the moral improvement of the child. If the parents are vicious, and themselves the cause of the child's bad character, they may not only be deprived of the care of the child, but may be treated as incorrigible, and sent to the correction establishments. Punishments in the schools are of three degrees—light, middling, and hard (*leicht, mittel, und schwer*). The instrument used is a cane. The first degree includes one or two strokes on the hand, the second up to four strokes, the third extends beyond four strokes, and includes punishments of posterior application. On the whole, corporal punishment is not more severe than in our own board schools, where there is now almost no ground for complaint. Punishment is never inflicted in such a manner as to degrade the child. It is characteristic of the schools of Berlin, as of German schools in general, that the aim always is to cultivate the self-respect of the pupils. Instead of corporal punishment, extra tasks are sometimes imposed, and the pupil is kept in school after hours; but this form of correction is becoming more rare.

Agreeable features of the school-work are the weekly or bi-weekly botanical and natural history excursions which pupils in the upper forms make with the teachers. Afternoon rambles among the woods surrounding the city, or in the Botanical or Zoological Gardens, where objects of interest are pointed out and described by the teachers, are among the most educative influences which the schools provide. In winter, when the fields and gardens afford no attractions, the Museums of Art and Industry present their treasures. It is one of the pleasantest sights to see groups of boys or girls gathered round their teacher, eagerly listening to his simple prelections on one specimen after another, as he conducts his band of little students over the collection. Who that has observed the numbers of poor children of a Saturday afternoon wandering aimlessly among the treasures in our Museums of Science and Art but has longed for some friendly guide to explain the objects that lie under the meaningless gaze of the little folk?

In Berlin there is a general School Museum for the benefit of teachers, where they may themselves get wider acquaintance, through books, apparatus, and specimens, with whatever branch of applied art they may wish to study, and so fit themselves to accompany the scholars with intelligence and interest on their museum explorations. In our large cities we have all the means for this kind of work, but we are slow to use them. We seem content for the present merely to possess some of the finest collections of industrial art specimens, without concerning ourselves to do anything to explain them to the crowds of young people who can only stare at them in vacant wonderment. We do not even attempt to place on the specimens an adequate printed description which might help to explain them.

Continuation schools are conducted for the benefit of lads and girls who have begun work on their own account. These schools not only afford the means of making up for lost time to young people who, through sickness or natural defect, have not been able to reach the highest class during their school years in the common schools, but they encourage the youths of better parts to keep up the habit of study, and so become more useful members of society. In these schools, which are open for part of the summer evenings as well as in winter, pupils are carried forward in the study of languages, chiefly French and English, in book-keeping, shorthand, drawing, and modelling. The number attending such schools is now nearly 8000.

But the Corporation maintain for the benefit of young workpeople another sort of school, of which we know too little in this country. These are trade schools (*Gewerbe - Schulen*), in which young artisans are instructed in the technicalities of the trade they have chosen, the use of their tools, and something of the science of their calling.[1] A house-painter will learn drawing and the elements of design, and obtain a knowledge of the chemical qualities of various colouring matters; a joiner will be instructed in the strength and properties of raw material and the application of different kinds of tools; even the barber is conducted through the higher walks of his art in the artificial uses of hair. Trade schools for saddlers, smiths, wheelmakers, shoemakers, glaziers, masons, and others, are open to young tradesmen, who, for a small fee of from two to four marks per session, may acquire much knowledge that cannot fail to make them better workmen, and that may also prove the foundation of future promotion. This branch of educational work was only started about ten years ago, but it has proved exceedingly useful. Its adoption

---

[1] In Edinburgh the Heriot-Watt Evening Schools do similar work.

is becoming general throughout the country, and other trades are being added to those which have already been embraced in the scheme. It is evident, as one studies the common aspects of German education, that it will be not merely a cheaper out-turn of German work with which we shall have to maintain competition in the future. Unless we give fuller attention to the technical instruction of our young working people, we shall be beaten where we have hitherto held the field, in the region of efficient workmanship.

Finally, the Corporation concern themselves with the education of the blind and of deaf-mute children — or, as they are pathetically named, children of four senses (*viersinnige*) — within the municipality. Except for very special reasons the city, while ready to give all needed assistance, will not take blind children from the care of their parents. It is felt that to keep blind children exclusively in the company of the blind is detrimental to their proper development, and that the more they mingle among seeing people, their mental faculties become keener and their interest in life fuller. But it is recognised that for the elements of education a special training is necessary, and accordingly a central school is maintained for the blind, where children are taught reading, writing, arithmetic, and music. Owing to the size of Berlin, the bringing of the children to school presents a somewhat serious problem. It is, however, solved partly by a system of tramcar passes, and partly by calling in the aid of the little orphan girls who are boarded by the Poor Administration in different parts of the city. These little women, on their way to the ordinary schools, call for the blind children in their neighbourhood, and conduct them to the institution and back—surely a kindly and humanising bit of service.

In connection with the school for the blind, there is a continuation school, where instruction in literature and in the theory and practice of music is given, and where boys are taught wicker-work, brush-making, and other arts, and the girls knitting and embroidery, with a view to their earning an independent living. In its whole treatment of the blind, the town aims at developing an independent spirit and the feeling that their want of sight should not exclude them in any great degree from the pleasures of life, while it need not inevitably increase its sadness.

The Corporation also maintain a separate institution for deaf-mutes. Here the children receive the same course of instruction as is followed in the common schools. It is to be noted that communication with the pupils is made exclusively by articulate speech—the children using the eye instead of the ear while attending to the teacher.

For the maintenance of its whole school establishments, higher schools, common schools, continuation schools, and the others now described, Berlin is this year expending over £680,000. About £100,000 is derived from fees paid by the higher scholars and from sundry other sources of revenue. In the common schools the annual cost is nearly 53s. per scholar. In the higher schools, after deduction of fees, it is 60s. per scholar. Over all, the scholars attending the municipal schools of all kinds cost the city annually about 54s. per head.

PUBLIC WORKS—FREE LIBRARY—FIRE-BRIGADE

CHAPTER VIII.

PUBLIC WORKS, FREE LIBRARY, FIRE-BRIGADE.

The Buildings Committee—Hobrecht's work—Functions of Committee—Frequent breaking-up of streets—How avoided—Public markets—Leaders of municipal improvement—Central market—District markets—Parks and gardens—The Thiergarten—School of forestry—Flowers for hospitals—Botanical specimens for schools—Public library—Branch libraries—Classes of readers—Fire-brigade—Its discipline—Its effectiveness—Samaritan Society.

ONE of the most important committees of the Corporation, and one which during the past twenty years has discharged most laborious duties, is that which is intrusted with the construction and oversight of the streets and public buildings (*Bau-Verwaltung*). It is composed of twenty-three members, partly councillors and partly magistrates, and it is presided over by one of the paid magistrates. It has been well for Berlin during the period of the rapid increase of its population that the entire business of supervising the laying out and construction of new streets has been committed to the care of one administration, and not to a number of vestries or district boards. The city is remarkable for the spaciousness of its streets, by which abundance of light and air is secured to the dwellings. Its roadways and footpaths are of superior make, and with its thirty miles of asphalted streets, it will compare favourably, in respect of its thoroughfares, with any European city. It is to Stadtrath Hobrecht, who for many years directed this department, that Berlin is chiefly indebted not only for the excellence of its streets, but for the splendid engineering of its drainage system, and for its consequent superiority as a place of residence. Herr Hobrecht, the Hausmann of Berlin, is the son of a Scottish mother, a Johnstone of Annandale, who belonged to Ecclefechan, Carlyle's native place, in Dumfriesshire; and he boasts that whatever energy he has been able to throw into his work he owes to his Scottish origin. The work of the department is divided into two classes—the buildings of municipal establishments (*Hochbau*) and the structure of streets and thoroughfares (*Tiefbau*). The building and structural maintenance of the public schools, hospitals, and other municipal institutions fall under the first class. The making and upkeep of the roadways, footpaths, bridges, and water-courses fall under the second. From their very nature, and from the constantly increasing numbers of the population, the labours of this department are onerous and incessant. Yet the whole work is carried on with admirable order and precision. It is extremely rare in Berlin to find the traffic of a whole thoroughfare blocked through the street undergoing repair. The streets are so wide that one side can generally be used while the other is being renewed. Moreover, the department takes care that whatever repairs may be necessary to drains, water-pipes, gas-pipes, or electric wires, shall be done at the same time that the street is under ordinary repair. Frequent breaking-up of streets is thus prevented, and economy is secured. The small percentage of loss of gas and water by leakage proves that the workmanship of the mains is of good quality, and that the opportunities for repairs while the street is broken for ordinary purposes are sufficient. No department of the service of the town more completely shows how the centralising of authority and responsibility can be made effective without interference with the proper work of other departments. Many departments have to make use of the streets in carrying on their own work, but on no account may any of them break ground without the previous sanction of the Streets and Buildings Committee. When the drainage, water, or other administrations apply for leave to open any street or footway, the Streets Committee notify the other departments which use the streets to ascertain whether in the vicinity of the proposed opening any other repairs are necessary, in order that all requisite work may be done at one disturbance of the traffic. Whatever street repairs or alterations are done by one department or another must be executed at the sight and to the satisfaction of the Streets Committee, who see to the proper laying and fitting of sewage, water, or other conduits, and to the proper finishing of tramway lines. The result is that the streets of the city are kept in excellent order, that the interruption of traffic through repairs is reduced to a minimum, and that the general management and control of the thoroughfares afford an excellent example to other towns on the Continent and in this country.

The Public Markets (*Markt Hallen*) of Berlin form a leading feature in the municipal economy. It has long been the aim of the civic authorities to bring the necessaries of life within reach of the inhabitants at the lowest possible prices. For this purpose the town has always given facilities, by the maintenance of a municipal market-place, for bringing producers and consumers into immediate contact. Till the present century was well advanced one central market sufficed for the community; but before 1850 the growth of the town rendered further extension of market accommodation an absolute necessity. The lumbering waggons from the farms near the city were no longer able to carry sufficient supplies for the wants of a population which had quadrupled in fifty years. Railways were beginning to accomplish what the farmers' carts were failing to perform. But the old market-place had become wholly inadequate to accommodate the supplies required by the rapidly growing city. During the third quarter of the century, though new extensions were projected, nothing was accomplished to meet the constantly increasing demands of the ever-growing population. Small middlemen sprang up in every quarter and made large profits in retailing provisions. Food was consequently dear, and the poorer classes found it hard to maintain a tolerable existence. But in the rejuvenation which came after the war of 1870-71, when the Corporation fairly set out on its campaign of reconstruction and renovation, the question of new market-places began to receive thorough handling. In this, as in other departments, the city was fortunate in possessing one member of the Corporation able to grapple with the work and carry it to a successful issue. If Virchow was the champion of public health, if Hobrecht brought energy and constructive skill to the department of streets and buildings, if Meubrink became the pioneer in the vast system of drainage and the redemption of waste land by sewage irrigation, to Stadtrath Blankenstein belongs the honour of having introduced a system of public market-places so well furnished and complete in their accommodation as to be adequate for the requirements of the city for many years to come. Great difficulties had to be surmounted in order to acquire convenient sites for the markets, and strenuous opposition was offered to Blankenstein's schemes by the small retailers who had been making large profits out of the necessities of the people. In due time, however, these difficulties were overcome, and the Berlin markets are now unique in their kind.

Besides the Central Market in the Alexandra Platz there are eleven large market-places in as many districts of the city, so that every inhabitant is within easy reach of abundance of fresh food at the most moderate prices of the day. Butcher-meat, fish, fruit, vegetables, flowers, and small household utensils are the principal commodities. Stalls are let out to farmers and other merchants who bring their produce direct from the country. The markets are all under cover and form immense well-ventilated halls, possessing for the most part abundant daylight, and being well lighted by gas at night. All market goods which enter the town by rail—and only a small part is now brought in by country waggons—are set down at the Central Market which adjoins the Alexandra Station. Supplies are thence carted off to the district markets. All the markets are open every week-day from eight in the morning till eight in the evening, and admission is free to all purchasers. As they were erected so they are upheld and managed at the cost of the Corporation. But the revenue from the shops and stalls is not only sufficient for the annual charges, including interest on capital outlay, but yields a fair sum towards reduction of debt. Strict supervision is maintained by the Markets Committee, assisted by the police. Unwholesome food is promptly seized, cleanliness is rigidly enforced, and all refuse is cleared away at least once a-day.

What Berlin lacks of natural beauty from

lying flat in a sandy plain, she has to a wonderful degree made up by her magnificent parks and gardens. These are under the care of a committee of the Corporation (*Verwaltung der städtischen Park Garten und Baum-Anlagen*). The principal park is the famous Thiergarten, stretching for two miles with a breadth of nearly a mile, and lying between the west of the city and the neighbouring imperial residence of Charlottenburg. It is the chief playground of the Berliners, and combines forest, meadow, lawn, and garden attractions. Here also are skating and boating ponds, and horse rides for the sportive, carriage drives for the invalid and indolent, and botanic and zoological gardens for the scientific. In other outskirts of the city there are also splendid parks, the Humboldthain, the Friedrichshain, and the new park at Treptow. Smaller parks and gardens adorn the city in various places; many of the principal streets are lined with trees — there are no fewer than 45,000 trees under the care of the Parks Committee — and the principal street of Berlin takes its well-known name from the rows of lime-trees which beautify it from end to end. Berlin vies with Edinburgh in the garden plots which give a charm to her squares and public places, and bring glimpses of rural loveliness into the heart of the town. The inhabitants take pride in preserving those beauty spots from harm, nor do they grudge the cost of maintaining them in constant freshness. An annual sum of about £30,000 is expended by the Parks and Gardens Administration, which is, after all, less in proportion to the population than is expended in Edinburgh, while it includes the upkeep of many gardens which in our principal streets and squares would be maintained by private contributions. It may be noted that the Administration follow a peculiar method in parcelling out work. They do not pay their workmen individually, but give off the work in portions to foremen, who undertake to perform each portion for a given sum. The foremen in turn hire gardeners and labourers to do the work at a fixed wage. Part of the work of the Committee is the maintenance of a School of Forestry and Horticulture. The hospitals and almshouses of the city are regularly supplied with flowers from the public gardens. It is also the duty of the Administration to furnish all the public schools with botanical specimens for purposes of demonstration in the class-rooms. Twice a-week each of the common schools receives from 100 to 150 specimens of each of four different kinds of plants, and every higher school receives as many specimens in each of eight different kinds. For the information of the teachers, the families, classes, and orders of the plants to be sent to the schools are set forth in a weekly municipal print.

The Corporation possess a public library; but for the present it can at best be described as only an admirable skeleton of a library. There is no central institution, but there are twenty-six district libraries with from 2000 to 8000 volumes in each. In each establishment there are a news-room, a reading-room for visitors using works of reference, and a lending department. The use of the libraries is free to the citizens. The library is maintained out of the common good of the town; but, when it is mentioned that little over £1000 per annum is expended on new books and rebindings, it will be seen that the undertaking is run on very thrifty principles. The total number of citizens using the books lent out does not yet exceed 15,000 per annum. A stand of about 110,000 volumes constitutes the whole establishment; but the works are of a more serious nature than those of most public libraries. The three-volume novel is hardly known in Berlin. What works of fiction there are consist chiefly of novels of an expository kind (*Tendenz Romane*). Your German reader of fiction prefers his novel to expound some philosophical or social idea worked out to a severely logical issue. No Scott or Dickens or Thackeray, no Hugo or Dumas, has yet arisen among the Germans. Wit, humour, and satire are exotics in German literature. Very ordinary fun goes a long way with the German reader; a book like Stinde's 'Buchholz Family,' for example, which contains rather more than ordinary fun, is sufficient to keep Berlin in laughter for a year. Thus, while half the library consists of works in general national literature, including of course the master-works of German poets and philosophers, it contains comparatively few works of a lighter sort. This should be kept in mind when we are comparing Berlin with places where the largest number of readers are those who make novels their chief mental relaxation. At the same time, Germany is better provided than any other nation with excellent translations of the best literature of foreign countries. For a few pence one may purchase a good translation of almost any of the best books of foreign authors. One may get any of George Eliot's novels for a shilling or little more; Ibsen's 'Peer Gynt,' which has recently made a sensation in an English version published at six shillings, has been current in Berlin for over ten years in a vigorous German rendering at the price of fourpence. Reading clubs for the study of the works of Shakespeare, Scott, Tennyson, Carlyle, George Eliot, Dickens, and Thackeray are common in Berlin, as they are also in other parts of the empire. The library is largely indebted to authors and publishers for additions to its stock. Careful note is kept of the different classes of readers, and of the departments of literature which they patronise. Women make a fourth part of the readers, and they read most in general literature. Students form another fourth, and they, more than any other class, read foreign and scientific books. Artisans, merchants, teachers, officials, and soldiers come next in order. There are no juvenile readers, or at least there is no department of the library specially assigned to them. The use of the library is eminently practical. It is far less a means of amusement and relaxation than of general culture and equipment for the business of life. Artisans and merchants use most of the technical works. Soldiers read books of travel, history, biography, but no theology; officials and teachers read the classics, foreign literature, economics, philosophy, and science. But the library is not yet a great popular resort. The framework is there, and it is, no doubt, destined to grow into one of the most beneficent institutions of Berlin. Meanwhile the Corporation do not venture to impose a Free Library rate upon the taxpayers. They are waiting for their Carnegie. With a gift of

£50,000 with such frugal methods as theirs, what would they not accomplish!

The municipal Fire-brigade is a sort of military institution, and the method of stopping conflagrations is reduced to a science. The brigade consists of nearly 900 men, with 120 horses, under the command of a firemaster-in-chief. It is divided into five companies, each consisting of about 180 men and 24 horses, and commanded by inspectors with the rank of commissioned officers. The men are classified into firemen proper and hosemen (*Feuermänner und Spritzenmänner*). There is a sergeant or foreman to every ten or twelve men. When a fire breaks out, one of the companies is instantly despatched to the spot, the police clear the ground and keep the public at a distance, the hosemen attach their pipes to the street hydrants, and line up along the hose lengths, delivering volumns of water at the fire with the precision of clockwork; the firemen stand attention, accoutrements in hand, ready at the word of command to spring in detachments into any part of the burning building to which they may be ordered. They are perfectly drilled and know their work; no shouting is heard save the quick, short orders of the officers. Prompt, alert movement and absolute order prevail, and usually the fire is subdued in a marvellously short time. Great fires are of comparatively rare occurrence in Berlin. This no doubt is mainly owing to the width of the streets and the consequent ease with which a fire can be reached, as well as to the efficient condition of the fire-brigade. Each of the five companies has a station of its own—one of these being also the brigade headquarters. Besides these principal stations, there are nine or ten sub-stations throughout the city, with telegraphic communication connecting the whole. The city is also provided with a complete system of fire-alarums, by which the central station is apprised of the locality of a fire the instant it is discovered. The minuteness with which the statistics of the department are recorded is amusing, but it is characteristic of the German passion for detail. Fires are described in three classes—great, middling, and small; the locality of the fire, the nature of the property involved, and the initial cause of the fire are not only fully set forth, but the most trifling accidents, even to the hurt of a finger or a slight abrasion on a horse's knee, and the subsequent treatment of the wound, are sedulously written down in the annual report. In connection with the department there is a Samaritan Society, whose special care is to give immediate attention to any one injured. There is also a Benevolent Fund, supported by insurance companies and persons whose property is saved by the brigade, for the benefit of widows and orphans of firemen and of members of the brigade who have been incapacitated by accident or old age.

POLICE—TREASURY—GENERAL POWERS OF CORPORATION

CHAPTER IX.

POLICE—TREASURY—POWERS OF CORPORATION.

Regular police force—maintained by State; Night watchmen—maintained by town; Police regulations — Advertising — Public clocks—Licensed houses—Drinking habits—Absence of drunkenness—Public conveyances—Tramcars—Treasury department—Finance Committee an advisory board—Influence on spending Committees—City accounts—Manner of spending public money — Liberality combined with frugality—Self-government in German towns—Powers of Corporation—Limitations—State authorities to sanction special works—Arbitration courts—Inexpensive procedure—No costly private bills.

THE police watching of the city is in two departments—the day watch and the night watch. The regular police, whose duty is to preserve the public peace, detect crime, and secure the apprehension of criminals, is solely under the control of the State. But the Corporation maintain a force of night watchmen, whose duty is mainly

K

to protect the property of the lieges. There is an old standing controversy between the town and the State as to the right of the former to control the whole police, but the State has strenuously adhered to the policy of keeping the full control of the regular police, which is an armed force, in its own hands, and of maintaining it solely out of the national revenues to which the citizens only contribute as Imperial taxpayers. On the other hand, the State bears no part of the cost of the night watchmen, who are maintained out of the local rates. It is the duty of the regular police to enforce all laws passed by the Corporation for the regulation of street traffic, the proper management of licensed places and the prevention of nuisances, and to bring to justice offenders against the public weal. In one particular a stranger observes a pleasing difference between the police regulations of Berlin and those other large towns — namely, in the entire absence of glaring advertisements and offensive sky-signs. In all the leading thoroughfares handsome clock pillars have recently been erected, which not merely serve to show the time of day, the weather forecasts and sidereal movements, but are extensively used as advertising mediums. By the clock arrangements, sets of tastefully displayed advertisements of all kinds are kept in constant motion, and passers-by may there read by day or by night—for the pillars are lighted by night—all they care to know about where they may buy the best wares, what entertainments are going on in the playhouses, and what sort of mustard, starch, or soap offers best value for their money.

All refreshment-houses are licensed, and proprietors are bound to keep strict order on their premises. Public-houses where alcoholic liquors are consumed usually supply cooked food likewise. A place where liquor alone is consumed is hardly to be found. The premises are generally large and open, and the box system is not tolerated. Drinking, it must be confessed, is general and deep, but drunkenness is not common. The proprietor of any house where a man had been allowed to make himself drunk would be warned by the police; a second offence would cost him his licence. With its teeming working-class population, Berlin is an example of sobriety to many cities in Britain. On festival days, or on occasions of large excursions to the country, nothing of the gross excess which marks such events among us is to be seen among the Berliners. There is a strong public opinion among the working-classes against drunkenness. Holidays are times of genuine enjoyment, and the luckless fellow who, through over-indulgence, has to be assisted home, forfeits the good opinion of his neighbours for a long time. The people are satisfied with light drinks which they can use in large quantities without intoxication. It is a consequence partly of education, partly, perhaps, of military discipline, but chiefly of the aversion to what is useless, which is a dominant quality of the modern German mind, that the people are so self-controlled. A man or a thing that is of no use to the community in Berlin is soon discarded.

Public conveyances are, of course, under police inspection; but cabs, omnibuses, and tramcars are all in the hands of private persons or companies. Berlin has an excellent tramway service, which, with the city railway, affords rapid and cheap conveyance to all parts. The tramway companies pay rent for the use of the streets, and their fares must be approved by the police department. When they require to repair their lines they must obtain the sanction of the Streets Committee, so that any other repairs falling to be done by the city may be executed at the same time. Passengers may not stop a tramcar at any point they please, but must mount or alight at appointed halting-places, which are marked at every few hundred yards along the thoroughfares. This arrangement implies care for the horses as well as for the avoidance of accidents.

The Treasury Department of Berlin is presided over by a Finance Committee (*Finanz-Deputation*), consisting of seventeen members, six of whom are magistrates. The treasurer, or chamberlain (*Kämmerer*), as he is called, is chairman of the committee. He is one of the paid magistrates, and holds office for a period of twelve years. He is head not only of the Finance Committee but of the whole permanent official staff. The work of the committee is to advise the magistracy and council in all matters affecting ways and means, the raising of new rates and the treatment of the municipal debt. The committee may claim the right to be heard by the magistracy on all new schemes involving more than ordinary expenditure. They are expected to show how far existing revenue is available for new proposals, and whether it is advisable to levy further rates or to allow certain items of proposed expenditure to stand over. The committee are, however, only advisory. The council, through the magistracy, accept full responsibility for voting municipal moneys, and it is not in the power of the Finance Committee to refuse supplies or to veto any outlay sanctioned by the council. Yet the surveillance exercised by the committee is of the healthiest kind. Whatever warnings they may address to the council, whatever representations regarding the laying out of money they may make either on grounds of economy or public policy, are received with respect. In the bureau of the permanent staff accounts are kept with such clearness and order that the committee can see from month to month how revenue and expenditure are coinciding with the estimates. They are thus able to give authoritative advice to the spending committees when occasion appears to call for it. The financial year commences on 31st March. The estimates made up by the various committees are ready for sanction by the council early in April; those for the current year are dated 8th April. The Berlin authorities do not like deficits, and, if the estimates err, it is on the side of fulness. In the preparation of them large use is made of the experience of past years. The spending committees have a wholesome habit of looking ahead and anticipating improvements likely to become necessary within a year or two. New projects form the subject of much deliberation before they are allowed to become a burden on the Treasury. Schemes put forward by different committees involving large outlay are considered in their relative importance, the more urgent always being preferred. The Finance Committee render great assistance to the council, not in dealing with the merits of such schemes—for upon the merits the council itself decides—but, as has been indicated, in showing to what extent such schemes may cause an increase upon the rates, and whether the occasion is favourable for an additional burden being laid upon the ratepayers. The book-keeping in the office department of the City Treasury is carried on in great detail and with praiseworthy simplicity. A sub-department, with a separate set of books, is assigned to each committee which has any charge of income or expenditure. The results shown by the different sets of books are carried to a principal set under the care of the upper officials. It is from the latter that a clear vidimus of the whole accounting can be promptly obtained.

It was observed at the outset that Berlin is not more heavily taxed for local purposes than Edinburgh, which bears a much lower burgh assessment than most of the large towns in Britain. But the remark deserves to be emphasised now that something has been learned about the return which Berlin is able to obtain for its taxation. No doubt the salaries of the higher officials are considerably less than with us. Skilled and educated labour is more abundant and consequently cheaper there than in Great Britain. It would be difficult to find an official drawing a salary of £100 a-year who had not passed a special examination previous to his appointment. Even the most ordinary officials are able to draw up intelligent and well-expressed reports on any part of their work. On the other hand, common labour is comparatively well paid by the Corporation, and it may be remembered that street-cleaners are almost as well paid in Berlin as they are here. The Corporation do not, however, imagine that to leave a department short of hands, or to get a piece of work done cheaply, is a sure saving of money. During the past twenty years they have emphatically shown that they regard generous expenditure on public works which make for the comfort and health of the community as justified by sound economy. But they take care to see their work done without waste or loss. All their departments are well manned, all their work is substantially and thoroughly done. Once an expenditure of money is proved to be needful, it is given without grudging; the Corporation never mistake niggardliness for economy. But a healthy frugality pervades the whole administration. No individual looking after his own affairs could be more vigilant to see that he gets the honest worth of his outlay than are the Corporation of Berlin, with their admirable system of departmental responsibility and their no less admirable method of concentrated magisterial supervision and control. There are few municipalities on whose scroll the famous Ciceronian maxim could be more appropriately inscribed—*Magnum vectigal est parsimonia.*

In bringing our observations to a close it only remains to point out the powers which belong to the Corporation, and under which they are able to carry out measures for the public wellbeing. Berlin, like all Prussian cities, has for many years enjoyed, within certain limitations, the right of self-government. In 1808 a law was passed which extended to all the towns of the old provinces of Prussia, and which settled once for all that those departments of public municipal affairs which had been previously managed by the State, should in future be worked by the town administrations. In other words, the supreme Government made over a part of its powers to the local government in the towns, to be exercised within the limits of the towns. It, however, reserved to itself the right of supervision over the local authorities. This right it exercises by making certain administrative acts of the towns dependent on State approval. The law of 1808 and subsequent extensions of that law have decreed which department of the State authority shall grant approval in particular cases. This authority, it is to be noted, can never be the Imperial Reichstag, for the Reichstag bears no direct official relationship to the towns of the confederation. Nor is it even the Prussian Parliament, for it is a constitutional principle in Prussia that the Parliament is not a ruling authority, but in reality only a factor in the promulgation of laws. The supervision rests solely with different State officers. In the smaller towns it is the Landrath, an official in some degree like the Sheriff-Substitute in Scotland, or the County Court Judge in England. In larger towns it is the President of the district, a functionary whose status corresponds to that of our Sheriffs-Principal or County Recorders. In Berlin, as an exceptional case, it is the Over-President or Lord Lieutenant of the Province of Brandenburg. In rare cases supervision is exercised by the Minister of the Interior, or Home Secretary. In only a few fast-disappearing instances, as, for example, in the choice of Bürgermeister or Ober-Bürgermeister, is the approval of the Emperor-King himself, as head of the Prussian State, required. The public law has, however, so well defined the province of local government, that cases in which State interference is necessary do not often occur. Especially is this so in the larger towns, where State sanction is practically confined to such matters as the issue of loans on the security of municipal rates. Upon a clear and fair representation of the case State sanction is never refused, except for strong reasons of public policy; and little or no expense is incurred in obtaining it. It is not required in matters purely affecting the proper administration of the town, such as drainage schemes, water-works, bridge-building, street extension within the boundaries, gas-works, or the erection of public buildings. The State has indeed set up an authority of its own within the largest towns—including Berlin—that, namely, of the police, the chief officials of which are in their way officers of State. The police department of Berlin is concerned not merely with the protection of life and property within the town, but a section of it is charged with the fulfilment of functions which in Scotland we are familiar with as exercised by Guild Courts. That is to say, it rests with this department to examine all plans for new buildings. The appointment of the officials of this section of the Police Department (*Polizei Verwaltung*) rests with the Minister of the Interior. Not only do buildings proposed to be erected by the town come under the cognisance of this authority, but all buildings, of whatsoever kind, proposed to be erected for public or private purposes. If, therefore, the Corporation wish to erect an asylum, school, or hospital, they must, like ordinary private persons, submit their plans to the Police Department, and obtain sanction before proceeding with the work. This can only be refused for architectural or sanitary reasons. In the three residence towns of Berlin, Potsdam, and Charlottenburg, there has been reserved to the Emperor-King the right of vetoing lines of street building and tramcar lines. As already remarked, the Corporation possess no tramcar system of their own, but let out the streets to private companies, which must obtain not only the right to use the streets, which are town property, but also the approval of the police authority, which is given only after the royal approval has been signified.

It is settled public law in Prussia—and it must be owned that the law is distinctly utilitarian in its conception—that owners of property hold it subject to the right of the State or the municipality to take it compulsorily, on due compensation, for any purpose in the public interest. If, then, the Corporation resolve to carry out some improvement—to cut a new street, erect a new institution, or make an extension of the drainage system—proprietors cannot refuse to sell their property if it be required for such purposes. The town, having obtained the necessary sanction from one or other of the authorities described, has a fixed period within which to exercise this right; or it may, for reasons of its own, renounce its right, or make no use of it. But the owner is always bound, and if the town require his property, he and the town must go before arbitration authorities (not law courts), who have experts to guide them, and who fix the full value to be paid for the property proposed to be taken. Both parties, the town and the owner, have the right to dispute the decisions of the arbitrators by a suit in the proper courts, but it is not often that these decisions are overturned. The full value of the property being duly ascertained and fixed, it must be instantly paid in hard cash. More than the full value is not paid. There is no *solatium* over and above full value. In this manner the whole of the vast expense with which we are so familiar in this country, incurred by corporations in promoting private bills in Parliament for carrying out measures of local improvement of the most obvious necessity, is wholly obviated. It is as if we had here in operation a public law, dispensing altogether with the irritating and expensive parliamentary proceedings at present in vogue, and leaving corporations and individuals precisely where they are after a Corporation Improvement Bill has been passed into law, with the Lands Clauses Act and other public statutes to guide parties to a settlement of whatever difference may be between them. This, assuredly, though the last, is not the least important lesson which we at home may learn from the municipality of Berlin.

INDEX.

	PAGE
Accounts, municipal—	
Range of,	10
Orderliness and clearness,	14
Advertisements, how regulated,	147
Annual expenditure,	11
Arbitration tribunals,	158
Authorities of State, when required,	156, 157
Bathing establishments,	84
Baths in private dwellings,	25
Benevolent fund (fire),	141
Berlin—	
Annual Civil expenditure,	16, 17
Capital of Hohenzollerns,	2
Historic interest less than other German towns,	2
Medical school,	69
Present importance,	3
Proposed enlargement of boundaries,	6
Rapid growth,	5
Within easy reach of Great Britain,	1
Blankenstein magistrate—	
His services to market department,	129
Blind, school for,	120, 121
" continuation school for,	121
Book-keeping at Treasury,	152
Botanising excursions,	116

	PAGE
Botanical gardens,	134, 135
" specimens for schools,	135
Brown-book, magisterial,	13, 80
Bürgermeister—	
A paid official,	7
How chosen,	7
Canals, connecting Spree and Oder,	5
Cattle-market,	60, 61
Cellar dwellings,	34, 37
Chairmen of Committees,	9
Charité Hospital,	71
Cholera visitation,	45
Cisterns, not required,	24
City Railway,	60, 149
Cleanliness of inhabitants,	46
Clock pillars,	147
Coals for gas-supply,	28
Company, gas,	27
" old water,	19, 20
Continuation schools,	118
Convalescent homes—	82
How justified,	83
Conveyances, regulation of public,	148
Corporation—	
Constitution of,	7
Control exercised by,	10, 70
Powers of,	155, 158
Cramming avoided,	110
Dalldorf Institution for idiots,	93

Deaf-mutes, school for, . 122
Debt of city— . . . 11
　How incurred, . . . 18
　Reduction of, . . . 18
Departmental reports, annual, 13
　" responsibility, 154
Destructors, absence of, . 42
Dirty inhabitants, treatment of, ... 53, 54
Disinfectants, use of, . . 43
Disinfection establishment, 87, 88
Drainage districts, . . 36
Drunkenness, rarity of, . 148
　" public opinion against, ... 148
Dwellings of the poor in former years, . . . 34

Edinburgh municipal rates, . 11
　" poor-rates, . . 101
　" water-rate, . . 26
Education, free, . . . 108
　" compulsory, . 108
Election, great, and relief of poor, . . 87, 88, 89
Electric light, . . . 30
Emperor-King—
　May disapprove election of Ober-Bürgermeister or Bürgermeister, . . . 7
　May veto lines of street, . 158
Estimates, municipal, . . 151

Filthy dwellings, not tolerated, ... 53
Finance Committee—
　An advisory board, . . 140
　Their functions, . 141, 142
Finance department—
　Sections for different committees, ... 152
Fire-brigade, . . 139, 140
Forestry, school of, . . 134
Friedrichshain Hospital, . 76
　" Park, . 133
Frugality of Corporation, 153, 154

Gas, waste by leakage, . . 29

Gas-supply, by Company, . 27
　" by Corporation, 28
　" cost of, . . 28
　" profits on, . . 29
Gill, Mr Henry, manager and engineer of water department, ... 21
Gymnasial schools, . . 108
Gymnastics, ... 112

Habitual offenders, . 93, 94
Health of city, present, . 36
Hobrecht, Stadtbaurath—
　His Scottish descent, . 126
　Value of his service, . 126, 130
Holidays, school, . . . 112
Hospital reports, . . . 80
Hospitaliten, the . . . 93
Hospitals, public, . . 70
Houseless poor, shelters for, 90, 95
Humboldthain, . . . 133

Imbecile institution at Dalldorf, ... 98
Immunity from recent cholera epidemic, ... 45
Income, taxation on, . . 12
Infectious diseases, treatment of, ... 71, 72
Insanitary state of Berlin in 1872, ... 35
Inspectors of schools, . . 106
Insurance against gas explosions, ... 29

Jewish scholars, . . . 114
Jews, special treatment of meat for, ... 62

Kanalisation, . . . 36
Korrigenden, the, . 55, 93

Lavatories for males, . . 44
　" for females, . . 44
Leakage of water and gas, . 127
Library, public, . . . 135
　" books in, . . 136
　" in districts, . . 135

INDEX. 163

Licensed houses, . . . 147
Literary club, . . . 137
Lighting of city, . . 27, 28
Lunatics, cost of, . . 98, 99
Lymph Institute, . . . 83

Magisterial report, . . 13
     " supervision, . 10
Magistrates—
  How chosen, . . . 8
  Half paid, half unpaid, . 8
  Number of, . . . 8
  Functions of, . . . 9
Manholes for drain inspection, ... 43
Manners of school children, . 113
Markets, public, 129, 130, 131
   " district, . . . 131
   " regulation of, . 132
Meat inspection, . 62, 63, 64, 65
Medical officers in hospitals, how paid, 80
   " " for relief of poor, . 91
Menbrink, Magistrate—
  His service to drainage system, . . . 5, 129
  On liberty of the subject, . 53
Microscopists, . . 63, 64
Moabit Hospital, . 72, 73, 74, 75
Mortality, former . . . 35
   " present, . . 36
Müggel Lake, . . . 19
Museum for teachers, . . 117
Museums, instruction in, . 116
Music, carefully cultivated, 112, 113

Natural history excursion, . 116
Night shelters for houseless, 95
  " watchmen, . . . 146
Nurses, male, . . . 81
Nursing staff in hospitals, . 81

Ober-Bürgermeister—
  A paid official, . . . 7
  How chosen, . . . 7
Orphan depot, . . 96, 97

Orphan houses, . . . 96
Outdoor relief, . . 91, 92

Paid magistrates, . . . 8
Parks, ... 133
Patients, cost of hospital, 78, 79
Pauperisation, Union for Prevention of, . 99, 100, 101
Police, maintained by State, 145, 146
Poor administration, . . 90
  " cost of, . . . 92
  " aged, ... 95
  " children, . . . 96
  " " boarding out of, 97
  " " education of, . 97
  " discrimination in relief of, 92
  " District Committees, . 91
  " medical relief, . 96, 98
  " visitation of, . . 91
Population, growth of, . . 5
Poverty, signs of, . . . 56
Private schools, . . 107, 108
Profits on gas, . . . 29
  " water, . . 12, 26
Property for municipal purposes, how acquired, . 159
Public debt, . . . 11, 18
  " health, Corporation's zeal for, . . . 51
  " schools, . . 107, 108
Pumping-stations, . . 37

Radial system of drainage, . 40
  " cost of, . . . 41
Rates, local, . . . 12
Registers at sewage tanks, 38, 39
Religious instruction, . . 114
Rental, taxation on, . . 12
Rieselfelder, ... 37
Rohrbeck's meat-disinfector, ... 64, 65

Sanitary condition, former, 33, 34, 35
  " " present, 36, 45
Scavengers, . . . 46, 47
School administration, . 105, 106

School, age of compulsory attendance, . . 109
" attendance, . 111, 114
" classes, . . 109, 110
" committees, . . 106
" inspectors, . . 106
" punishments, . 115, 116
Schools, common, . 107, 109
" cost of, . . . 122
" fees in higher, 108, 122
" higher for boys, . 107
" higher for girls, . 107
" modern for boys, . 108
Self-government in Berlin, . 155
Sewage, fields for utilisation of, ... 37
Sewage-fields, cost of, . . 41
" " three kinds, . 39
" " profits from, . 40
Shelters for the houseless, . 54
Siemens' meters, . . . 23
Slaughter-houses . . 61, 62
Slums, absence of, . . 52
Sobriety, general, . . . 148
" causes of, . . 148
Socialism, centre of, . . 56
Spree connecting Elbe and Oder, ... 3
Squalor, absence of, . . 57
State supervision, . . 154, 155
Street-cleaning, . . . 41
" refuse, how dealt with, 42, 43
" repairs, . . . 127
" " regulation of, 128
Streets, asphalted, . . 41
" committee, . . 125

Tanks for collection of drainage, ... 36
Taxation, ... 12
Tegel Lake, ... 19
Thiergarten, ... 133
Town Council—
  Committees of, . . . 7
  Functions of, . . . 8
  How elected, . . . 8
  Number of members, . 8

Trade, extent of, . . . 3
" schools, . . 118, 119
Tramways, ... 12
Traps in street drains, . . 43
Treasurer of city, . . . 149
Treasury bureau, . . . 150
Trees in Berlin, . . . 133
Treptow Park, . . . 133

Urban Hospital, . . 77, 78
Union for Prevention of Pauperisation, . . 99, 101
Unter den Linden, . . 4

Ventilation of drains, . . 43
Veterinary staff for meat inspection, . . . 63
Victoria Training Institution for Nurses, . . . 82
Virchow—
  His service to Berlin, . 34
  Pleads for improved sanitation, . . . 35, 58
  Report to Town Council in 1872, ... 35
Visitation of poor, . . 91

Waste-land reclaimed by sewage, ... 37
Watering of streets, . . 45
Water apparatus, . . 23, 24
" channels, . . . 43
" closets, general in private dwellings, . 25
" engineer, . . . 21
" meters, . . 21, 22
" profits on supply of, 12, 26
" supply per head, . 25
" waste of, . . . 22
" works, . . . 19
Water-supply by old company, . . . 19, 20
" taken over by Corporation, . . . 19
Working-class population, . 56

Zelle, Ober-Bürgermeister, . 8

Catalogue

of

Messrs Blackwood & Sons' Publications

PHILOSOPHICAL CLASSICS FOR ENGLISH READERS.

Edited by WILLIAM KNIGHT, LL.D.,
Professor of Moral Philosophy in the University of St Andrews.

In crown 8vo Volumes, with Portraits, price 3s. 6d.

Contents of the Series.

Descartes, by Professor Mahaffy, Dublin.—Butler, by Rev. W. Lucas Collins, M.A.—Berkeley, by Professor Campbell Fraser.—Fichte, by Professor Adamson, Owens College, Manchester.—Kant, by Professor Wallace, Oxford.—Hamilton, by Professor Veitch, Glasgow.—Hegel, by Professor Edward Caird, Glasgow.—Leibniz, by J. Theodore Merz.—Vico, by Professor Flint, Edinburgh.—Hobbes, by Professor Croom Robertson.—Hume, by the Editor.—Spinoza, by the Very Rev. Principal Caird, Glasgow.—Bacon: Part I. The Life, by Professor Nichol.—Bacon: Part II. Philosophy, by the same Author.—Locke, by Professor Campbell Fraser.

FOREIGN CLASSICS FOR ENGLISH READERS.

Edited by Mrs OLIPHANT.

In crown 8vo, 2s. 6d.

Contents of the Series

Dante, by the Editor.—Voltaire, by General Sir E. B. Hamley, K.C.B.—Pascal, by Principal Tulloch.—Petrarch, by Henry Reeve, C.B.—Goethe, by A. Hayward, Q.C.—Molière, by the Editor and F. Tarver, M.A.—Montaigne, by Rev. W. L. Collins, M.A.—Rabelais, by Walter Besant, M.A.—Calderon, by E. J. Hasell.—Saint Simon, by Clifton W. Collins, M.A.—Cervantes, by the Editor.—Corneille and Racine, by Henry M. Trollope.—Madame de Sévigné, by Miss Thackeray.—La Fontaine, and other French Fabulists, by Rev. W. Lucas Collins, M.A.—Schiller, by James Sime, M.A., Author of 'Lessing, his Life and Writings.'—Tasso, by E. J. Hasell.—Rousseau, by Henry Grey Graham.—Alfred de Musset, by C. F. Oliphant.

ANCIENT CLASSICS FOR ENGLISH READERS.

Edited by the Rev. W. LUCAS COLLINS, M.A.

Complete in 28 Vols. crown 8vo, cloth, price 2s. 6d. each. And may also be had in 14 Volumes, strongly and neatly bound, with calf or vellum back, £3, 10s.

Contents of the Series.

Homer: The Iliad, by the Editor.—Homer: The Odyssey, by the Editor.—Herodotus, by George C. Swayne, M.A.—Xenophon, by Sir Alexander Grant, Bart., LL.D.—Euripides, by W. B. Donne.—Aristophanes, by the Editor.—Plato, by Clifton W. Collins, M.A.—Lucian, by the Editor.—Æschylus, by the Right Rev. the Bishop of Colombo.—Sophocles, by Clifton W. Collins, M.A.—Hesiod and Theognis, by the Rev. J. Davies, M.A.—Greek Anthology, by Lord Neaves.—Virgil, by the Editor.—Horace, by Sir Theodore Martin, K.C.B.—Juvenal, by Edward Walford, M.A.—Plautus and Terence, by the Editor—The Commentaries of Cæsar, by Anthony Trollope.—Tacitus, by W. B. Donne.—Cicero, by the Editor.—Pliny's Letters, by the Rev. Alfred Church, M.A., and the Rev. W. J. Brodribb, M.A.—Livy, by the Editor.—Ovid, by the Rev. A. Church, M.A.—Catullus, Tibullus, and Propertius, by the Rev. Jas. Davies, M.A.—Demosthenes, by the Rev. W. J. Brodribb, M.A.—Aristotle, by Sir Alexander Grant, Bart., LL.D.—Thucydides, by the Editor.—Lucretius, by W. H. Mallock, M.A.—Pindar, by the Rev. F. D. Morice, M.A.

Saturday Review.—"It is difficult to estimate too highly the value of such a series as this in giving 'English readers' an insight, exact as far as it goes, into those olden times which are so remote, and yet to many of us so close."

CATALOGUE

OF

MESSRS BLACKWOOD & SONS'

PUBLICATIONS.

ALISON.
    History of Europe. By Sir ARCHIBALD ALISON, Bart., D.C.L.
        1. From the Commencement of the French Revolution to the Battle of Waterloo.
            LIBRARY EDITION, 14 vols., with Portraits. Demy 8vo, £10, 10s.
            ANOTHER EDITION, in 20 vols. crown 8vo, £6.
            PEOPLE'S EDITION, 13 vols. crown 8vo, £2, 11s.
        2. Continuation to the Accession of Louis Napoleon.
            LIBRARY EDITION, 8 vols. 8vo, £6, 7s. 6d.
            PEOPLE'S EDITION, 8 vols. crown 8vo, 34s.
    Epitome of Alison's History of Europe. Thirtieth Thousand, 7s. 6d.
    Atlas to Alison's History of Europe. By A. Keith Johnston.
        LIBRARY EDITION, demy 4to, £3, 3s.
        PEOPLE'S EDITION, 31s. 6d.
    Life of John Duke of Marlborough. With some Account of his Contemporaries, and of the War of the Succession. Third Edition. 2 vols. 8vo. Portraits and Maps, 30s.
    Essays: Historical, Political, and Miscellaneous. 3 vols. demy 8vo, 45s.

ACROSS FRANCE IN A CARAVAN: BEING SOME ACCOUNT OF A JOURNEY FROM BORDEAUX TO GENOA IN THE "ESCARGOT," taken in the Winter 1889-90. By the Author of 'A Day of my Life at Eton.' With fifty Illustrations by John Wallace, after Sketches by the Author, and a Map. Demy 8vo, 15s.

ACTA SANCTORUM HIBERNIÆ; Ex Codice Salmanticensi. Nunc primum integre edita opera CAROLI DE SMEDT et JOSEPHI DE BACKER, e Soc. Jesu, Hagiographorum Bollandianorum; Auctore et Sumptus Largiente JOANNE PATRICIO MARCHIONE BOTHAE. In One handsome 4to Volume, bound in half roxburghe, £2, 2s.; in paper cover, 31s. 6d.

AGRICULTURAL HOLDINGS ACT, 1883. With Notes by a MEMBER OF THE HIGHLAND AND AGRICULTURAL SOCIETY. 8vo, 5s. 6d.

AIKMAN.
    Manures and the Principles of Manuring. By C. M. AIKMAN, B.Sc., F.R.S.E., &c. Lecturer on Agricultural Chemistry, West of Scotland Technical College; Examiner in Chemistry, University of Glasgow. Crown 8vo.
                                                                 [Shortly.

AIKMAN.
  Farmyard Manure: Its Nature, Composition, and Treatment. Crown 8vo, 1s. 6d.

AIRD. Poetical Works of Thomas Aird. Fifth Edition, with Memoir of the Author by the Rev. JARDINE WALLACE, and Portrait. Crown 8vo, 7s. 6d.

ALLARDYCE.
  The City of Sunshine. By ALEXANDER ALLARDYCE. Three vols. post 8vo, £1, 5s. 6d.

  Memoir of the Honourable George Keith Elphinstone, K.B., Viscount Keith of Stonehaven, Marischal, Admiral of the Red. 8vo, with Portrait, Illustrations, and Maps, 21s.

ALMOND. Sermons by a Lay Head-master. By HELY HUTCHINSON ALMOND, M.A. Oxon., Head-master of Loretto School. Crown 8vo, 5s.

ANCIENT CLASSICS FOR ENGLISH READERS. Edited by Rev. W. LUCAS COLLINS, M.A. Price 2s. 6d. each. *For List of Vols., see p. 2.*

ANNALS OF A FISHING VILLAGE. By "A SON OF THE MARSHES." *See page 28.*

AYTOUN.
  Lays of the Scottish Cavaliers, and other Poems. By W. EDMONDSTOUNE AYTOUN, D.C.L., Professor of Rhetoric and Belles-Lettres in the University of Edinburgh. New Edition. Fcap. 8vo, 3s. 6d.
    ANOTHER EDITION. Fcap. 8vo, 7s. 6d.
    CHEAP EDITION. 1s. Cloth, 1s. 3d.

  An Illustrated Edition of the Lays of the Scottish Cavaliers. From designs by Sir NOEL PATON. Small 4to, in gilt cloth, 21s.

  Bothwell: a Poem. Third Edition. Fcap., 7s. 6d.

  Poems and Ballads of Goethe. Translated by Professor AYTOUN and Sir THEODORE MARTIN, K.C.B. Third Edition. Fcap., 6s.

  Bon Gaultier's Book of Ballads. By the SAME. Fifteenth Edition. With Illustrations by Doyle, Leech, and Crowquill. Fcap. 8vo, 5s.

  The Ballads of Scotland. Edited by Professor AYTOUN. Fourth Edition. 2 vols. fcap. 8vo, 12s.

  Memoir of William E. Aytoun, D.C.L. By Sir THEODORE MARTIN, K.C.B. With Portrait. Post 8vo, 12s.

BACH.
  On Musical Education and Vocal Culture. By ALBERT B. BACH. Fourth Edition. 8vo, 7s. 6d.

  The Principles of Singing. A Practical Guide for Vocalists and Teachers. With Course of Vocal Exercises. Crown 8vo, 6s.

  The Art of Singing. With Musical Exercises for Young People. Crown 8vo, 3s.

  The Art Ballad: Loewe and Schubert. With Music Illustrations. With a Portrait of LOEWE. Third Edition. Small 4to, 5s.

BAIRD LECTURES.
  Theism. By Rev. Professor FLINT, D.D., Edinburgh. Eighth Edition. Crown 8vo, 7s. 6d.

  Anti-Theistic Theories. By Rev. Professor FLINT, D.D., Edinburgh. Fourth Edition. Crown 8vo, 10s. 6d.

BAIRD LECTURES.

The Early Religion of Israel. As set forth by Biblical Writers and modern Critical Historians. By Rev. Professor ROBERTSON, D.D., Glasgow. Third Edition. Crown 8vo, 10s. 6d.

The Inspiration of the Holy Scriptures. By Rev. ROBERT JAMIESON, D.D. Crown 8vo, 7s. 6d.

The Mysteries of Christianity. By Rev. Professor CRAWFORD, D.D. Crown 8vo, 7s. 6d.

Endowed Territorial Work: Its Supreme Importance to the Church and Country. By Rev. WILLIAM SMITH, D.D. Crown 8vo, 6s.

BALLADS AND POEMS. By MEMBERS OF THE GLASGOW BALLAD CLUB. Crown 8vo, 7s. 6d.

BANNATYNE. Handbook of Republican Institutions in the United States of America. Based upon Federal and State Laws, and other reliable sources of information. By DUGALD J. BANNATYNE, Scotch Solicitor, New York; Member of the Faculty of Procurators, Glasgow. Crown 8vo, 7s. 6d.

BELLAIRS.

The Transvaal War, 1880-81. Edited by Lady BELLAIRS. With a Frontispiece and Map. 8vo, 15s.

Gossips with Girls and Maidens, Betrothed and Free. New Edition. Crown 8vo, 3s. 6d. Cloth, extra gilt edges, 5s.

BELLESHEIM. History of the Catholic Church of Scotland. From the Introduction of Christianity to the Present Day. By ALPHONS BELLESHEIM, D.D., Canon of Aix-la-Chapelle. Translated, with Notes and Additions, by D. OSWALD HUNTER BLAIR, O.S.B., Monk of Fort Augustus. Complete in 4 vols. demy 8vo, with Maps. Price 12s. 6d. each.

BENTINCK. Racing Life of Lord George Cavendish Bentinck, M.P., and other Reminiscences. By JOHN KENT, Private Trainer to the Goodwood Stable. Edited by the Hon. FRANCIS LAWLEY. With Twenty-three full-page Plates, and Facsimile Letter. Second Edition. Demy 8vo, 25s.

BESANT.

The Revolt of Man. By WALTER BESANT. Tenth Edition. Crown 8vo, 3s. 6d.

Readings in Rabelais. Crown 8vo, 7s. 6d.

BEVERIDGE.

Culross and Tulliallan; or Perthshire on Forth. Its History and Antiquities. With Elucidations of Scottish Life and Character from the Burgh and Kirk-Session Records of that District. By DAVID BEVERIDGE. 2 vols. 8vo, with Illustrations, 42s.

Between the Ochils and the Forth; or, From Stirling Bridge to Aberdour. Crown 8vo, 6s.

BIRCH.

Examples of Stables, Hunting-Boxes, Kennels, Racing Establishments, &c. By JOHN BIRCH, Architect, Author of 'Country Architecture,' &c. With 30 Plates. Royal 8vo, 7s.

Examples of Labourers' Cottages, &c. With Plans for Improving the Dwellings of the Poor in Large Towns. With 34 Plates. Royal 8vo, 7s.

Picturesque Lodges. A Series of Designs for Gate Lodges, Park Entrances, Keepers', Gardeners', Bailiffs', Grooms', Upper and Under Servants' Lodges, and other Rural Residences. With 16 Plates. 4to, 12s. 6d.

BLACK. Heligoland and the Islands of the North Sea. By WILLIAM GEORGE BLACK. Crown 8vo, 4s.

BLACKIE.

Lays and Legends of Ancient Greece. By JOHN STUART BLACKIE, Emeritus Professor of Greek in the University of Edinburgh. Second Edition. Fcap. 8vo, 5s.

The Wisdom of Goethe. Fcap. 8vo. Cloth, extra gilt, 6s.

Scottish Song: Its Wealth, Wisdom, and Social Significance. Crown 8vo. With Music. 7s. 6d.

A Song of Heroes. Crown 8vo, 6s.

BLACKMORE.
The Maid of Sker. By R. D. BLACKMORE, Author of 'Lorna Doone,' &c. New Edition. Crown 8vo, 6s.

BLACKWOOD.

Blackwood's Magazine, from Commencement in 1817 to December 1892. Nos. 1 to 926, forming 152 Volumes.

Index to Blackwood's Magazine. Vols. 1 to 50. 8vo, 15s.

Tales from Blackwood. First Series. Price One Shilling each, in Paper Cover. Sold separately at all Railway Bookstalls. They may also be had bound in 12 vols., cloth, 18s. Half calf, richly gilt, 30s. Or the 12 vols. in 6, roxburghe, 21s. Half red morocco, 28s.

Tales from Blackwood. Second Series. Complete in Twenty-four Shilling Parts. Handsomely bound in 12 vols., cloth, 30s. In leather back, roxburghe style, 37s. 6d. Half calf, gilt, 52s. 6d. Half morocco, 55s.

Tales from Blackwood. Third Series. Complete in Twelve Shilling Parts. Handsomely bound in 6 vols., cloth, 15s.; and in 12 vols., cloth, 18s. The 6 vols. in roxburghe, 21s. Half calf, 25s. Half morocco, 28s.

Travel, Adventure, and Sport. From 'Blackwood's Magazine.' Uniform with 'Tales from Blackwood.' In Twelve Parts, each price 1s. Handsomely bound in 6 vols., cloth, 15s. And in half calf, 25s.

New Educational Series. *See separate Catalogue.*

New Uniform Series of Novels (Copyright). Crown 8vo, cloth. Price 3s. 6d. each. Now ready:—

KATIE STEWART, and other Stories. By Mrs Oliphant.
VALENTINE, AND HIS BROTHER. By the Same.
SONS AND DAUGHTERS. By the Same.
MARMORNE. By P. G. Hamerton.
REATA. By E. D. Gerard.
BEGGAR MY NEIGHBOUR. By the Same.
THE WATERS OF HERCULES. By the Same.
FAIR TO SEE. By L. W. M. Lockhart.
MINE IS THINE. By the Same.
DOUBLES AND QUITS. By the Same.
HURRISH. By the Hon. Emily Lawless.
ALTIORA PETO. By Laurence Oliphant.
PICCADILLY. By the Same. With Illustrations.
THE REVOLT OF MAN. By Walter Besant.
LADY BABY. By D. Gerard.
THE BLACKSMITH OF VOE. By Paul Cushing.
THE DILEMMA. By the Author of 'The Battle of Dorking.'
MY TRIVIAL LIFE AND MISFORTUNE. By A Plain Woman.
POOR NELLIE. By the Same.

Others in preparation.

Standard Novels. Uniform in size and binding. Each complete in one Volume.

FLORIN SERIES, Illustrated Boards. Bound in Cloth, 2s. 6d.

TOM CRINGLE'S LOG. By Michael Scott.
THE CRUISE OF THE MIDGE. By the Same.
CYRIL THORNTON. By Captain Hamilton.
ANNALS OF THE PARISH. By John Galt.
THE PROVOST, &c. By the Same.
SIR ANDREW WYLIE. By the Same.
THE ENTAIL. By the Same.
MISS MOLLY. By Beatrice May Butt.
REGINALD DALTON. By J. G. Lockhart.
PEN OWEN. By Dean Hook.
ADAM BLAIR. By J. G. Lockhart.
LADY LEE'S WIDOWHOOD. By General Sir E. B. Hamley.
SALEM CHAPEL. By Mrs Oliphant.
THE PERPETUAL CURATE. By the Same.
MISS MARJORIBANKS. By the Same.
JOHN: A Love Story. By the Same.

BLACKWOOD. Standard Novels.

SHILLING SERIES, Illustrated Cover. Bound in Cloth, 1s. 6d.

THE RECTOR, and THE DOCTOR'S FAMILY. By Mrs Oliphant.
THE LIFE OF MANSIE WAUCH. By D. M. Moir.
PENINSULAR SCENES AND SKETCHES. By F. Hardman.
SIR FRIZZLE PUMPKIN, NIGHTS AT MESS, &c.
THE SUBALTERN.
LIFE IN THE FAR WEST. By G. F. Ruxton.
VALERIUS: A Roman Story. By J. G. Lockhart.

BOLTON. Lord Wastwater. A Novel. By SIDNEY BOLTON. 2 vols. crown 8vo, 17s.

BON GAULTIER'S BOOK OF BALLADS. Fifteenth Edition. With Illustrations by Doyle, Leech, and Crowquill. Fcap. 8vo, 5s.

BONNAR. Biographical Sketch of George Meikle Kemp, Architect of the Scott Monument, Edinburgh. By THOMAS BONNAR, F.S.A. Scot., Author of 'The Present Art Revival,' 'The Past of Art in Scotland,' 'Suggestions for the Picturesque of Interiors,' &c. With Three Portraits and numerous Illustrations. Post 8vo, 7s. 6d.

BOSCOBEL TRACTS. Relating to the Escape of Charles the Second after the Battle of Worcester, and his subsequent Adventures. Edited by J. HUGHES, Esq., A.M. A New Edition, with additional Notes and Illustrations, including Communications from the Rev. R. H. BARHAM, Author of the 'Ingoldsby Legends.' 8vo, with Engravings, 16s.

BROUGHAM. Memoirs of the Life and Times of Henry Lord Brougham. Written by HIMSELF. 3 vols. 8vo, £2, 8s. The Volumes are sold separately, price 16s. each.

BROWN. A Manual of Botany, Anatomical and Physiological. For the Use of Students. By ROBERT BROWN, M.A., Ph.D. Crown 8vo, with numerous Illustrations, 12s. 6d.

BROWN. The Book of the Landed Estate. Containing Directions for the Management and Development of the Resources of Landed Property. By ROBERT E. BROWN, Factor and Estate Agent. Royal 8vo, with Illustrations, 21s.

BROWN. The Forester: A Practical Treatise on the Planting, Rearing, and General Management of Forest-trees. By JAMES BROWN, LL.D., Inspector of and Reporter on Woods and Forests. Fifth Edition, Revised and Enlarged. Royal 8vo, with Engravings, 36s.

BRUCE. In Clover and Heather. Poems by WALLACE BRUCE. New and Enlarged Edition. Crown 8vo, 4s. 6d.
A limited number of Copies of the First Edition, on large hand-made paper, 12s. 6d.

BRYDALL. Art in Scotland; its Origin and Progress. By ROBERT BRYDALL, Master of St George's Art School of Glasgow. 8vo, 12s. 6d.

BUCHAN. Introductory Text-Book of Meteorology. By ALEXANDER BUCHAN, LL.D., F.R.S.E., Secretary of the Scottish Meteorological Society, &c. Crown 8vo, with 8 Coloured Charts and Engravings, 4s. 6d.

BUCHANAN. The Shiré Highlands (East Central Africa). By JOHN BUCHANAN, Planter at Zomba. Crown 8vo, 5s.

BURBIDGE.
Domestic Floriculture, Window Gardening, and Floral Decorations. Being practical directions for the Propagation, Culture, and Arrangement of Plants and Flowers as Domestic Ornaments. By F. W. BURBIDGE. Second Edition. Crown 8vo, with numerous Illustrations, 7s. 6d.

Cultivated Plants: Their Propagation and Improvement. Including Natural and Artificial Hybridisation, Raising from Seed, Cuttings, and Layers, Grafting and Budding, as applied to the Families and Genera in Cultivation. Crown 8vo, with numerous Illustrations, 12s. 6d.

BURROWS. Commentaries on the History of England, from the Earliest Times to 1865. By MONTAGU BURROWS, Chichele Professor of Modern History in the University of Oxford; Captain R.N.; F.S.A., &c.; "Officier de l'Instruction Publique" of France. Crown 8vo, 7s. 6d.

BURTON.

The History of Scotland: From Agricola's Invasion to the Extinction of the last Jacobite Insurrection. By JOHN HILL BURTON, D.C.L., Historiographer-Royal for Scotland. New and Enlarged Edition, 8 vols., and Index. Crown 8vo, £3, 3s.

History of the British Empire during the Reign of Queen Anne. In 3 vols. 8vo. 36s.

The Scot Abroad. Third Edition. Crown 8vo, 10s. 6d.

The Book-Hunter. New Edition. With Portrait. Crown 8vo, 7s. 6d.

BUTE.

The Roman Breviary: Reformed by Order of the Holy Œcumenical Council of Trent; Published by Order of Pope St Pius V.; and Revised by Clement VIII. and Urban VIII.; together with the Offices since granted. Translated out of Latin into English by JOHN, Marquess of Bute, K.T. In 2 vols. crown 8vo, cloth boards, edges uncut. £2, 2s.

The Altus of St Columba. With a Prose Paraphrase and Notes. In paper cover, 2s. 6d.

BUTLER. Pompeii: Descriptive and Picturesque. By W. BUTLER. Post 8vo, 5s.

BUTT.

Miss Molly. By BEATRICE MAY BUTT. Cheap Edition, 2s.

Eugenie. Crown 8vo, 6s. 6d.

Elizabeth, and other Sketches. Crown 8vo, 6s.

Delicia. New Edition. Crown 8vo, 2s. 6d.

CAIRD.

Sermons. By JOHN CAIRD, D.D., Principal of the University of Glasgow. Sixteenth Thousand. Fcap. 8vo, 5s.

Religion in Common Life. A Sermon preached in Crathie Church, October 14, 1855, before Her Majesty the Queen and Prince Albert. Published by Her Majesty's Command. Cheap Edition, 3d.

CALDER. Chaucer's Canterbury Pilgrimage. Epitomised by WILLIAM CALDER. With Photogravure of the Pilgrimage Company, and other Illustrations, Glossary, &c. Crown 8vo, 4s.

CAMPBELL. Critical Studies in St Luke's Gospel: Its Demonology and Ebionitism. By COLIN CAMPBELL, D.D., Minister of the Parish of Dundee, formerly Scholar and Fellow of Glasgow University. Author of the 'Three First Gospels in Greek, arranged in parallel columns.' Post 8vo, 7s. 6d.

CAMPBELL. Sermons Preached before the Queen at Balmoral. By the Rev. A. A. CAMPBELL, Minister of Crathie. Published by Command of Her Majesty. Crown 8vo, 4s. 6d.

CAMPBELL. Records of Argyll. Legends, Traditions, and Recollections of Argyllshire Highlanders, collected chiefly from the Gaelic. With Notes on the Antiquity of the Dress, Clan Colours, or Tartans of the Highlanders. By Lord ARCHIBALD CAMPBELL. Illustrated with Nineteen full-page Etchings. 4to, printed on hand-made paper, £3, 3s.

CAMPBELL, W. D., AND V. K. ERSKINE. The Bailie M'Phee: A Curling Song. With Illustrations, and the Music to which it may be sung. Small 4to, 1s. 6d.

CANTON. A Lost Epic, and other Poems. By WILLIAM CANTON. Crown 8vo, 5s.

CARRICK. Koumiss; or, Fermented Mare's Milk: and its uses in the Treatment and Cure of Pulmonary Consumption, and other Wasting Diseases. With an Appendix on the best Methods of Fermenting Cow's Milk. By GEORGE L. CARRICK, M.D., L.R.C.S.E. and L.R.C.P.E., Physician to the British Embassy, St Petersburg, &c. Crown 8vo, 10s. 6d.

CARSTAIRS. British Work in India. By R. CARSTAIRS. Crown 8vo, 6s.

CAUVIN. A Treasury of the English and German Languages. Compiled from the best Authors and Lexicographers in both Languages. By JOSEPH CAUVIN, LL.D. and Ph.D., of the University of Göttingen, &c. Crown 8vo, 7s. 6d.

CAVE-BROWN. Lambeth Palace and its Associations. By J. CAVE-BROWN, M.A., Vicar of Detling, Kent, and for many years Curate of Lambeth Parish Church. With an Introduction by the Archbishop of Canterbury. Second Edition, containing an additional Chapter on Medieval Life in the Old Palaces. 8vo, with Illustrations, 21s.

CHARTERIS. Canonicity; or, Early Testimonies to the Existence and Use of the Books of the New Testament. Based on Kirchhoffer's 'Quellensammlung.' Edited by A. H. CHARTERIS, D.D., Professor of Biblical Criticism in the University of Edinburgh. 8vo, 18s.

CHRISTISON. Life of Sir Robert Christison, Bart., M.D., D.C.L. Oxon., Professor of Medical Jurisprudence in the University of Edinburgh. Edited by his SONS. In 2 vols. 8vo. Vol. I.—Autobiography. 16s. Vol. II.—Memoirs. 16s.

CHRONICLES OF STRATHEDEN. A Highland Parish of To-day. By a Resident. Crown 8vo, 5s.

CHRONICLES OF WESTERLY: A Provincial Sketch. By the Author of 'Culmshire Folk,' 'John Orlebar,' &c. 3 vols. crown 8vo, 25s. 6d.

CHURCH SERVICE SOCIETY.
A Book of Common Order: being Forms of Worship issued by the Church Service Society. Sixth Edition. Crown 8vo, 6s. Also in 2 vols. crown 8vo, 6s. 6d.

Order of Divine Service for Children. Issued by the Church Service Society. With Scottish Hymnal. Cloth, 3d.

CLELAND. Too Apt a Pupil. By ROBERT CLELAND, Author of 'Barbara Allan, the Provost's Daughter.' Crown 8vo, 6s.

CLOUSTON. Popular Tales and Fictions: their Migrations and Transformations. By W. A. CLOUSTON, Editor of 'Arabian Poetry for English Readers,' &c. 2 vols. post 8vo, roxburghe binding, 25s.

COCHRAN. A Handy Text-Book of Military Law. Compiled chiefly to assist Officers preparing for Examination; also for all Officers of the Regular and Auxiliary Forces. Comprising also a Synopsis of part of the Army Act. By Major F. COCHRAN, Hampshire Regiment Garrison Instructor, North British District. Crown 8vo, 7s. 6d.

COLQUHOUN. The Moor and the Loch. Containing Minute Instructions in all Highland Sports, with Wanderings over Crag and Corrie, Flood and Fell. By JOHN COLQUHOUN. Seventh Edition. With Illustrations. Demy 8vo, 21s.

CONSTITUTION AND LAW OF THE CHURCH OF SCOTLAND. With an Introductory Note by the late Principal Tulloch. New Edition, Revised and Enlarged. Crown 8vo, 3s. 6d.

CONSTITUTIONAL YEAR BOOK. Published annually. Paper cover, 1s.; cloth, 1s. 6d.

COTTERILL. Suggested Reforms in Public Schools. By C. C. COTTERILL, M.A. Crown 8vo, 3s. 6d.

CRANSTOUN.
The Elegies of Albius Tibullus. Translated into English Verse, with Life of the Poet, and Illustrative Notes. By JAMES CRANSTOUN, LL.D., Author of a Translation of 'Catullus.' Crown 8vo, 6s. 6d.

The Elegies of Sextus Propertius. Translated into English Verse, with Life of the Poet, and Illustrative Notes. Crown 8vo, 7s. 6d.

CRAWFORD. An Atonement of East London, and other Poems. By HOWARD CRAWFORD, M.A. Crown 8vo, 5s.

CRAWFORD. Saracinesca. By F. MARION CRAWFORD, Author of 'Mr Isaacs,' &c. &c. Sixth Edition. Crown 8vo, 6s.

CRAWFORD.
The Doctrine of Holy Scripture respecting the Atonement. By the late THOMAS J. CRAWFORD, D.D., Professor of Divinity in the University of Edinburgh. Fifth Edition. 8vo, 12s.

The Fatherhood of God, Considered in its General and Special Aspects. Third Edition, Revised and Enlarged. 8vo, 9s.

The Preaching of the Cross, and other Sermons. 8vo, 7s. 6d.

The Mysteries of Christianity. Crown 8vo, 7s. 6d.

CROSS. Impressions of Dante, and of the New World; with a Few Words on Bimetallism. By J. W. CROSS, Editor of 'George Eliot's Life, as related in her Letters and Journals.' Post 8vo. [*Immediately.*]

CUSHING.
The Blacksmith of Voe. By PAUL CUSHING, Author of 'The Bull i' th' Thorn,' 'Cut with his own Diamond.' Cheap Edition. Crown 8vo, 3s. 6d.

DAVIES.
Norfolk Broads and Rivers; or, The Waterways, Lagoons, and Decoys of East Anglia. By G. CHRISTOPHER DAVIES. Illustrated with Seven full-page Plates. New and Cheaper Edition. Crown 8vo, 6s.

Our Home in Aveyron. Sketches of Peasant Life in Aveyron and the Lot. By G. CHRISTOPHER DAVIES and Mrs BROUGHALL. Illustrated with full-page Illustrations. 8vo, 15s. Cheap Edition, 7s. 6d.

DE LA WARR. An Eastern Cruise in the 'Edeline.' By the Countess DE LA WARR. In Illustrated Cover. 2s.

DESCARTES. The Method, Meditations, and Principles of Philosophy of Descartes. Translated from the Original French and Latin. With a New Introductory Essay, Historical and Critical, on the Cartesian Philosophy. By Professor VEITCH, LL.D., Glasgow University. Tenth Edition. 6s. 6d.

DEWAR. Voyage of the "Nyanza," R.N.Y.C. Being the Record of a Three Years' Cruise in a Schooner Yacht in the Atlantic and Pacific, and her subsequent Shipwreck. By J. CUMMING DEWAR, late Captain King's Dragoon Guards and 11th Prince Albert's Hussars. With Two Autogravures, numerous Illustrations, and a Map. Demy 8vo, 21s.

DICKSON. Gleanings from Japan. By W. G. DICKSON, Author of 'Japan: Being a Sketch of its History, Government, and Officers of the Empire.' With Illustrations. 8vo, 16s.

DILEMMA, The. By the Author of 'The Battle of Dorking.' New Edition. Crown 8vo, 3s. 6d.

DOGS, OUR DOMESTICATED: Their Treatment in reference to Food, Diseases, Habits, Punishment, Accomplishments. By 'MAGENTA.' Crown 8vo, 2s. 6d.

DOMESTIC EXPERIMENT, A. By the Author of 'Ideala: A Study from Life.' Crown 8vo, 6s.

DOUGLAS. Chinese Stories. By ROBERT K. DOUGLAS. With numerous Illustrations by Parkinson, Forestier, and others. Small demy 8vo, 12s. 6d.

DU CANE. The Odyssey of Homer, Books I.-XII. Translated into English Verse. By Sir CHARLES DU CANE, K.C.M.G. 8vo, 10s. 6d.

DUDGEON. History of the Edinburgh or Queen's Regiment Light Infantry Militia, now 3rd Battalion The Royal Scots; with an Account of the Origin and Progress of the Militia, and a Brief Sketch of the Old Royal Scots. By Major R. C. DUDGEON, Adjutant 3rd Battalion the Royal Scots. Post 8vo, with Illustrations, 10s. 6d.

DUNCAN. Manual of the General Acts of Parliament relating to the Salmon Fisheries of Scotland from 1828 to 1882. By J. BARKER DUNCAN. Crown 8vo, 5s.

DUNSMORE. Manual of the Law of Scotland as to the Relations between Agricultural Tenants and the Landlords, Servants, Merchants, and Bowers. By W. DUNSMORE. 8vo, 7s. 6d.

DUPRÈ. Thoughts on Art, and Autobiographical Memoirs of Giovanni Dupré. Translated from the Italian by E. M. PERUZZI, with the permission of the Author. New Edition. With an Introduction by W. W. STORY. Crown 8vo, 10s. 6d.

ELIOT.
    George Eliot's Life, Related in Her Letters and Journals. Arranged and Edited by her husband, J. W. CROSS. With Portrait and other Illustrations. Third Edition. 3 vols. post 8vo, 42s.

    George Eliot's Life. (Cabinet Edition.) With Portrait and other Illustrations. 3 vols. crown 8vo, 15s.

    George Eliot's Life. With Portrait and other Illustrations. New Edition, in one volume. Crown 8vo, 7s. 6d.

    Works of George Eliot (Cabinet Edition). 21 volumes, crown 8vo, price £5, 5s. Also to be had handsomely bound in half and full calf. The Volumes are sold separately, bound in cloth, price 5s. each—viz.: Romola. 2 vols.—Silas Marner, The Lifted Veil, Brother Jacob. 1 vol.—Adam Bede. 2 vols.—Scenes of Clerical Life. 2 vols.—The Mill on the Floss. 2 vols.—Felix Holt. 2 vols.—Middlemarch. 3 vols.—Daniel Deronda. 3 vols.—The Spanish Gypsy. 1 vol.—Jubal, and other Poems, Old and New. 1 vol.—Theophrastus Such. 1 vol.—Essays. 1 vol.

    Novels by George Eliot. Cheap Edition. Adam Bede. Illustrated. 3s. 6d., cloth.—The Mill on the Floss. Illustrated. 3s. 6d., cloth.—Scenes of Clerical Life. Illustrated. 3s., cloth.—Silas Marner: the Weaver of Raveloe. Illustrated. 2s. 6d., cloth.—Felix Holt, the Radical. Illustrated. 3s. 6d., cloth.—Romola. With Vignette. 3s. 6d., cloth.

    Middlemarch. Crown 8vo, 7s. 6d.

    Daniel Deronda. Crown 8vo, 7s. 6d.

    Essays. New Edition. Crown 8vo, 5s.

    Impressions of Theophrastus Such. New Edition. Crown 8vo, 5s.

    The Spanish Gypsy. New Edition. Crown 8vo, 5s.

    The Legend of Jubal, and other Poems, Old and New. New Edition. Crown 8vo, 5s.

    Wise, Witty, and Tender Sayings, in Prose and Verse. Selected from the Works of GEORGE ELIOT. Eighth Edition. Fcap. 8vo, 6s.

ELIOT.
  The George Eliot Birthday Book. Printed on fine paper, with red border, and handsomely bound in cloth, gilt. Fcap. 8vo, 3s. 6d. And in French morocco or Russia, 5s.

  ESSAYS ON SOCIAL SUBJECTS. Originally published in the 'Saturday Review.' New Edition. First and Second Series. 2 vols. crown 8vo, 6s. each.

FAITHS OF THE WORLD, The. A Concise History of the Great Religious Systems of the World. By various Authors. Crown 8vo, 5s.

FARRER. A Tour in Greece in 1880. By RICHARD RIDLEY FARRER. With Twenty-seven full-page Illustrations by Lord WINDSOR. Royal 8vo, with a Map, 21s.

FERRIER.
  Philosophical Works of the Late James F. Ferrier, B.A. Oxon., Professor of Moral Philosophy and Political Economy, St Andrews. New Edition. Edited by Sir ALEXANDER GRANT, Bart., D.C.L., and Professor LUSHINGTON. 3 vols. crown 8vo, 34s. 6d.

  Institutes of Metaphysic. Third Edition. 10s. 6d.

  Lectures on the Early Greek Philosophy. 4th Edition. 10s. 6d.

  Philosophical Remains, including the Lectures on Early Greek Philosophy. New Edition. 2 vols., 24s.

FITZROY. Dogma and the Church of England. By A. I. FITZROY. Post 8vo, 7s. 6d.

FLINT.
  The Philosophy of History in Europe. By ROBERT FLINT, D.D., LL.D., Professor of Divinity, University of Edinburgh. 3 vols. 8vo.
  [New Edition in preparation. Vol. I.—FRANCE. Immediately.

  Agnosticism. Being the Croall Lecture for 1887-88.
  [In the press.

  Theism. Being the Baird Lecture for 1876. Eighth Edition, Revised. Crown 8vo, 7s. 6d.

  Anti-Theistic Theories. Being the Baird Lecture for 1877. Fourth Edition. Crown 8vo, 10s. 6d.

FORBES. Insulinde: Experiences of a Naturalist's Wife in the Eastern Archipelago. By Mrs H. O. FORBES. Crown 8vo, with a Map. 4s. 6d.

FOREIGN CLASSICS FOR ENGLISH READERS. Edited by Mrs OLIPHANT. Price 2s. 6d. For List of Volumes published, see page 2.

FOSTER. The Fallen City, and other Poems. By WILL FOSTER. Crown 8vo, 6s.

FRANCILLON. Gods and Heroes; or, The Kingdom of Jupiter. By R. E. FRANCILLON. With 8 Illustrations. Crown 8vo, 5s.

FULLARTON. Merlin: A Dramatic Poem. By RALPH MACLEOD FULLARTON. Crown 8vo, 5s.

GALT. Novels by JOHN GALT. Fcap. 8vo, boards, each 2s.; cloth, 2s. 6d.
  ANNALS OF THE PARISH.—THE PROVOST.—SIR ANDREW WYLIE.—THE ENTAIL.

GENERAL ASSEMBLY OF THE CHURCH OF SCOTLAND.
> Scottish Hymnal, With Appendix Incorporated. Published for use in Churches by Authority of the General Assembly. 1. Large type, cloth, red edges, 2s. 6d.; French morocco, 4s. 2. Bourgeois type, limp cloth, 1s.; French morocco, 2s. 3. Nonpareil type, cloth, red edges, 6d.; French morocco, 1s. 4d. 4. Paper covers, 3d. 5. Sunday-School Edition, paper covers, 1d.; cloth, 2d. No. 1, bound with the Psalms and Paraphrases, French morocco, 8s. No. 2, bound with the Psalms and Paraphrases, cloth, 2s.; French morocco, 3s.
>
> Prayers for Social and Family Worship. Prepared by a Special Committee of the General Assembly of the Church of Scotland. Entirely New Edition, Revised and Enlarged. Fcap. 8vo, red edges, 2s.
>
> Prayers for Family Worship. A Selection of Four Weeks' Prayers. New Edition. Authorised by the General Assembly of the Church of Scotland. Fcap. 8vo, red edges, 1s. 6d.

GERARD.
> Reata: What's in a Name. By E. D. GERARD. Cheap Edition. Crown 8vo, 3s. 6d.
>
> Beggar my Neighbour. Cheap Edition. Crown 8vo, 3s. 6d.
>
> The Waters of Hercules. Cheap Edition. Crown 8vo, 3s. 6d.

GERARD.
> The Land beyond the Forest. Facts, Figures, and Fancies from Transylvania. By E. GERARD. With Maps and Illustrations. 2 vols. post 8vo, 25s.
>
> Bis: Some Tales Retold. Crown 8vo, 6s.
>
> A Secret Mission. 2 vols. crown 8vo, 17s.

GERARD.
> Lady Baby. By DOROTHEA GERARD. Cheap Edition. Crown 8vo, 3s. 6d.
>
> Recha. Second Edition. Crown 8vo, 6s.

GERARD. Stonyhurst Latin Grammar. By Rev. JOHN GERARD. Second Edition. Fcap. 8vo, 3s.

GILL.
> Free Trade: an Inquiry into the Nature of its Operation. By RICHARD GILL. Crown 8vo, 7s. 6d.
>
> Free Trade under Protection. Crown 8vo, 7s. 6d.

GOETHE. Poems and Ballads of Goethe. Translated by Professor AYTOUN and Sir THEODORE MARTIN, K.C.B. Third Edition. Fcap. 8vo, 6s.

GOETHE'S FAUST. Translated into English Verse by Sir THEODORE MARTIN, K.C.B. Part I. Second Edition, post 8vo, 6s. Ninth Edition, fcap., 3s. 6d. Part II. Second Edition, Revised. Fcap. 8vo, 6s.

GORDON CUMMING.
> At Home in Fiji. By C. F. GORDON CUMMING. Fourth Edition, post 8vo. With Illustrations and Map. 7s. 6d.
>
> A Lady's Cruise in a French Man-of-War. New and Cheaper Edition. 8vo. With Illustrations and Map. 12s. 6d.
>
> Fire-Fountains. The Kingdom of Hawaii: Its Volcanoes, and the History of its Missions. With Map and Illustrations. 2 vols. 8vo, 25s.
>
> Wanderings in China. New and Cheaper Edition. 8vo, with Illustrations, 10s.
>
> Granite Crags: The Yō-semité Region of California. Illustrated with 8 Engravings. New and Cheaper Edition. 8vo, 8s. 6d.

GRAHAM. The Life and Work of Syed Ahmed Khan, C.S.I.
By Lieut.-Colonel G. F. I. GRAHAM, B.S.C. 8vo, 14s.

GRAHAM. Manual of the Elections (Scot.) (Corrupt and Illegal Practices) Act, 1890. With Analysis, Relative Act of Sederunt, Appendix containing the Corrupt Practices Acts of 1883 and 1885, and Copious Index. By J. EDWARD GRAHAM, Advocate. 8vo, 4s. 6d.

GRANT. Bush-Life in Queensland. By A. C. GRANT. New Edition. Crown 8vo, 6s.

GUTHRIE-SMITH. Crispus: A Drama. By H. GUTHRIE-SMITH. Fcap. 4to, 5s.

HAINES. Unless! A Romance. By RANDOLPH HAINES. Crown 8vo, 6s.

HALDANE. Subtropical Cultivations and Climates. A Handy Book for Planters, Colonists, and Settlers. By R. C. HALDANE. Post 8vo, 9s.

HALLETT. A Thousand Miles on an Elephant in the Shan States. By HOLT S. HALLETT, M. Inst. C.E., F.R.G.S., M.R.A.S., Hon. Member Manchester and Tyneside Geographical Societies. 8vo, with Maps and numerous Illustrations, 21s.

HAMERTON.
  Wenderholme: A Story of Lancashire and Yorkshire Life. By P. G. HAMERTON, Author of 'A Painter's Camp.' Crown 8vo, 6s.
  Marmorne. New Edition. Crown 8vo, 3s. 6d.

HAMILTON.
  Lectures on Metaphysics. By Sir WILLIAM HAMILTON, Bart., Professor of Logic and Metaphysics in the University of Edinburgh. Edited by the Rev. H. L. MANSEL, B.D., LL.D., Dean of St Paul's; and JOHN VEITCH, M.A., LL.D., Professor of Logic and Rhetoric, Glasgow. Seventh Edition. 2 vols. 8vo, 24s.
  Lectures on Logic. Edited by the SAME. Third Edition, Revised. 2 vols., 24s.
  Discussions on Philosophy and Literature, Education and University Reform. Third Edition. 8vo, 21s.
  Memoir of Sir William Hamilton, Bart., Professor of Logic and Metaphysics in the University of Edinburgh. By Professor VEITCH, of the University of Glasgow. 8vo, with Portrait, 18s.
  Sir William Hamilton: The Man and his Philosophy. Two Lectures delivered before the Edinburgh Philosophical Institution, January and February 1883. By Professor VEITCH. Crown 8vo, 2s.

HAMLEY.
  The Operations of War Explained and Illustrated. By General Sir EDWARD BRUCE HAMLEY, K.C.B., K.C.M.G. Fifth Edition, Revised throughout. 4to, with numerous Illustrations, 30s.
  National Defence; Articles and Speeches. Post 8vo, 6s.
  Shakespeare's Funeral, and other Papers. Post 8vo, 7s. 6d.
  Thomas Carlyle: An Essay. Second Edition. Crown 8vo, 2s. 6d.
  On Outposts. Second Edition. 8vo, 2s.
  Wellington's Career; A Military and Political Summary. Crown 8vo, 2s.
  Lady Lee's Widowhood. Crown 8vo, 2s. 6d.
  Our Poor Relations. A Philozoic Essay. With Illustrations, chiefly by Ernest Griset. Crown 8vo, cloth gilt, 3s. 6d.

HAMLEY. Guilty, or Not Guilty? A Tale. By Major-General W. G. HAMLEY, late of the Royal Engineers. New Edition. Crown 8vo, 3s. 6d.

HARRISON. The Scot in Ulster. The Story of the Scottish Settlement in Ulster. By JOHN HARRISON, Author of 'Oure Tounis Colledge.' Crown 8vo, 2s. 6d.

HASELL.
  Bible Partings. By E. J. HASELL. Crown 8vo, 6s.
  Short Family Prayers. Cloth, 1s.

HAY. Arakan: Past—Present—Future. A Resumé of Two Campaigns for its Development. By JOHN OGILVY HAY, J.P. ('Old Arakan'), Formerly Honorary Magistrate of the town of Akyab, Author of 'Indo-Burmah-China Railway Connections a Pressing Necessity.' With a Map. Demy 8vo, 4s. 6d.

HAY. The Works of the Right Rev. Dr George Hay, Bishop of Edinburgh. Edited under the Supervision of the Right Rev. Bishop STRAIN. With Memoir and Portrait of the Author. 5 vols. crown 8vo, bound in extra cloth, £1, 1s. The following Volumes may be had separately—viz.:
  The Devout Christian Instructed in the Law of Christ from the Written Word. 2 vols., 8s.—The Pious Christian Instructed in the Nature and Practice of the Principal Exercises of Piety. 1 vol., 3s.

HEATLEY.
  The Horse-Owner's Safeguard. A Handy Medical Guide for every Man who owns a Horse. By G. S. HEATLEY, M.R.C.V.S. Crown 8vo, 5s.
  The Stock-Owner's Guide. A Handy Medical Treatise for every Man who owns an Ox or a Cow. Crown 8vo, 4s. 6d.

HEDDERWICK.
  Lays of Middle Age; and other Poems. By JAMES HEDDERWICK, LL.D. Price 3s. 6d.
  Backward Glances; or, Some Personal Recollections. With a Portrait. Post 8vo, 7s. 6d.

HEMANS.
  The Poetical Works of Mrs Hemans. Copyright Editions. Royal 8vo, 5s. The Same with Engravings, cloth, gilt edges, 7s. 6d.
  Select Poems of Mrs Hemans. Fcap., cloth, gilt edges, 3s.

HERKLESS. Cardinal Beaton: Priest and Politician. By JOHN HERKLESS, Minister of Tannadice. With a Portrait. Post 8vo, 7s. 6d.

HOME PRAYERS. By Ministers of the Church of Scotland and Members of the Church Service Society. Second Edition. Fcap. 8vo, 3s.

HOMER.
  The Odyssey. Translated into English Verse in the Spenserian Stanza. By PHILIP STANHOPE WORSLEY. 3d Edition. 2 vols. fcap., 12s.
  The Iliad. Translated by P. S. WORSLEY and Professor CONINGTON. 2 vols. crown 8vo, 21s.

HUTCHINSON. Hints on the Game of Golf. By HORACE G. HUTCHINSON. Seventh Edition, Enlarged. Fcap. 8vo, cloth, 1s.

IDDESLEIGH.
  Lectures and Essays. By the late EARL of IDDESLEIGH, G.C.B., D.C.L., &c. 8vo, 16s.
  Life, Letters, and Diaries of Sir Stafford Northcote, First Earl of Iddesleigh. By ANDREW LANG. With Three Portraits and a View of Pynes. Third Edition. 2 vols. post 8vo, 31s. 6d.
    POPULAR EDITION. With Portrait and View of Pynes. Post 8vo, 7s. 6d.

INDEX GEOGRAPHICUS: Being a List, alphabetically arranged, of the Principal Places on the Globe, with the Countries and Subdivisions of the Countries in which they are situated, and their Latitudes and Longitudes. Imperial 8vo, pp. 676, 21s.

JEAN JAMBON. Our Trip to Blunderland ; or, Grand Excursion to Blundertown and Back. By JEAN JAMBON. With **Sixty** Illustrations designed by CHARLES DOYLE, engraved by DALZIEL. Fourth **Thousand**. Cloth, gilt edges, 6s. 6d. Cheap Edition, cloth, 3s. 6d. Boards, 2s. 6d.

JENNINGS. Mr Gladstone: A Study. By LOUIS J. JENNINGS, M.P., Author of 'Republican Government in the United States,' 'The Croker Memoirs,' &c. Popular Edition. Crown 8vo, 1s.

JERNINGHAM.
    Reminiscences of an Attaché. By HUBERT E. H. JERNINGHAM. Second Edition. Crown 8vo, 5s.
    Diane de Breteuille. A Love Story. Crown 8vo, 2s. 6d.

JOHNSTON.
    The Chemistry of Common Life. By Professor J. F. W. JOHNSTON. New Edition, Revised. By ARTHUR HERBERT CHURCH, M.A. Oxon.; Author of 'Food: its Sources, Constituents, and Uses,' &c. With Maps and 102 Engravings. Crown 8vo, 7s. 6d.
    Elements of Agricultural Chemistry. An entirely New Edition from the Edition by Sir CHARLES A. CAMERON, M.D., F.R.C.S.I., &c. Revised and brought down to date by C. M. AIKMAN, M.A., B.Sc., F.R.S.E., Lecturer on Agricultural Chemistry, West of Scotland Technical College. Fcap. 8vo. [*In preparation.*]
    Catechism of Agricultural Chemistry. An entirely New Edition from the Edition by Sir CHARLES A. CAMERON. Revised and Enlarged by C. M. AIKMAN, M.A., &c. 92d Thousand. With numerous Illustrations. Crown 8vo, 1s.

JOHNSTON. Patrick Hamilton: a Tragedy of the Reformation in Scotland, 1528. By T. P. JOHNSTON. Crown 8vo, with Two Etchings. 5s.

JOHNSTON. Agricultural Holdings (Scotland) Acts, 1883 and 1889; and the Ground Game Act, 1880. With Notes, and Summary of Procedure, &c. By CHRISTOPHER N. JOHNSTON, M.A., Advocate. Demy 8vo, 5s.

KEBBEL. The Old and the New: English Country Life. By T. E. KEBBEL, M.A, Author of 'The Agricultural Labourers,' 'Essays in History and Politics,' 'Life of Lord Beaconsfield.' Crown 8vo, 5s.

KENNEDY. Sport, Travel, and Adventure in Newfoundland and the West Indies. By Captain W. R. KENNEDY, R.N. With Illustrations by the Author. Post 8vo, 14s.

KING. The Metamorphoses of Ovid. Translated in English Blank Verse. By HENRY KING, M.A., Fellow of Wadham College, Oxford, and of the Inner Temple, Barrister-at-Law. Crown 8vo, 10s. 6d.

KINGLAKE.
    History of the Invasion of the Crimea. By A. W. KINGLAKE. Cabinet Edition, Revised. With an Index to the Complete Work. Illustrated with Maps and Plans. Complete in 9 vols., crown 8vo, at 6s. each.
    History of the Invasion of the Crimea. Demy 8vo. Vol. VI. Winter Troubles. With a Map, 16s. Vols. VII. and VIII. From the Morrow of Inkerman to the Death of Lord Raglan. With an Index to the Whole Work. With Maps and Plans. 28s.
    Eothen. A New Edition, uniform with the Cabinet Edition of the 'History of the Invasion of the Crimea.' 6s.

KNEIPP. My Water-Cure. As Tested through more than Thirty Years, and Described for the Healing of Diseases and the Preservation of Health. By SEBASTIAN KNEIPP, Parish Priest of Wörishofen (Bavaria). With a Portrait and other Illustrations. Authorised English Translation from the Thirtieth German Edition, by A. de F. Crown 8vo, 5s.

KNOLLYS. The Elements of Field-Artillery. Designed for the Use of Infantry and Cavalry Officers. By HENRY KNOLLYS, Captain Royal Artillery; Author of 'From Sedan to Saarbrück,' Editor of 'Incidents in the Sepoy War,' &c. With Engravings. Crown 8vo, 7s. 6d.

LAMINGTON. In the Days of the Dandies. By the late Lord LAMINGTON. Crown 8vo. Illustrated cover, 1s.; cloth, 1s. 6d.

LANG. Life, Letters, and Diaries of Sir Stafford Northcote, First Earl of Iddesleigh. By ANDREW LANG. With Three Portraits and a View of Pynes. Third Edition. 2 vols. post 8vo, 31s. 6d.
    POPULAR EDITION. With Portrait and View of Pynes. Post 8vo, 7s. 6d.

LAWLESS. Hurrish: A Study. By the Hon. EMILY LAWLESS, Author of 'A Chelsea Householder,' &c. Fourth Edition. Crown 8vo, 3s. 6d.

LEES. A Handbook of the Sheriff and Justice of Peace Small Debt Courts. With Notes, References, and Forms. By J. M. Lees, Advocate, Sheriff-Substitute of Lanarkshire. 8vo, 7s. 6d.

LIGHTFOOT. Studies in Philosophy. By the REV. J. LIGHTFOOT, M.A., D.Sc.; Vicar of Cross Stone, Todmorden. Crown 8vo, 4s. 6d.

LINDSAY. The Progressiveness of Modern Christian Thought. By the Rev. JAMES LINDSAY, M.A., B.D., B.Sc., F.R.S.E., F.G.S., Minister of the Parish of St Andrews, Kilmarnock. Crown 8vo, 6s.

LLOYD. Ireland under the Land League. A Narrative of Personal Experiences. By CLIFFORD LLOYD, Special Resident Magistrate. Post 8vo, 6s.

LOCKHART.
    Doubles and Quits. By LAURENCE W. M. LOCKHART. New Edition. Crown 8vo, 3s. 6d.
    Fair to See. New Edition. Crown 8vo, 3s. 6d.
    Mine is Thine. New Edition. Crown 8vo, 3s. 6d.

LOCKHART. The Church of Scotland in the Thirteenth Century. The Life and Times of David de Bernham of St Andrews (Bishop), A.D. 1239 to 1253. With List of Churches dedicated by him, and Dates. By WILLIAM LOCKHART, A.M., F.S.A. Scot., Minister of Colinton Parish. 2d Edition 8vo, 6s.

LORIMER.
    The Institutes of Law: A Treatise of the Principles of Jurisprudence as determined by Nature. By the late JAMES LORIMER, Professor of Public Law and of the Law of Nature and Nations in the University of Edinburgh. New Edition, Revised and much Enlarged. 8vo, 18s.
    The Institutes of the Law of Nations. A Treatise of the Jural Relation of Separate Political Communities. In 2 vols. 8vo. Volume I., price 16s. Volume II., price 20s.

LOVE. Scottish Church Music. Its Composers and Sources. With Musical Illustrations. By JAMES LOVE. Post 8vo, 7s. 6d.

M'COMBIE. Cattle and Cattle-Breeders. By WILLIAM M'COMBIE, Tillyfour. New Edition, Enlarged, with Memoir of the Author by JAMES MACDONALD, of the 'Farming World.' Crown 8vo, 3s. 6d.

M'CRIE.
    Works of the Rev. Thomas M'Crie, D.D. Uniform Edition. 4 vols. crown 8vo, 24s.

M'CRIE.
- Life of John Knox. Crown 8vo, 6s. Another Edition, 3s. 6d.
- Life of Andrew Melville. Crown 8vo, 6s.
- History of the Progress and Suppression of the Reformation in Italy in the Sixteenth Century. Crown 8vo, 4s.
- History of the Progress and Suppression of the Reformation in Spain in the Sixteenth Century. Crown 8vo, 3s. 6d.
- Lectures on the Book of Esther. Fcap. 8vo, 5s.

M'CRIE. The Public Worship of Presbyterian Scotland. Historically treated. With copious Notes, Appendices, and Index. The Fourteenth Series of the Cunningham Lectures. By the Rev. CHARLES G. M'CRIE. Demy 8vo, 10s. 6d.

MACDONALD. A Manual of the Criminal Law (Scotland) Procedure Act, 1887. By NORMAN DORAN MACDONALD. Revised by the LORD JUSTICE-CLERK. 8vo, 10s. 6d.

MACDONALD.
- History of Polled Aberdeen and Angus Cattle. Giving an Account of the Origin, Improvement, and Characteristics of the Breed. By JAMES MACDONALD and JAMES SINCLAIR, Sub-Editor 'Irish Farmer's Gazette.' Illustrated with numerous Animal Portraits. Post 8vo, 12s. 6d.
- Stephens Book of the Farm. Fourth Edition. Revised and in great part Rewritten by JAMES MACDONALD of the 'Farming World.' Complete in 3 vols., bound with leather back, gilt top, £3, 3s. In Six Divisions, bound in cloth, each 10s. 6d.
- Pringle's Live Stock of the Farm. Third Edition. Revised and Edited by JAMES MACDONALD. Crown 8vo, 7s. 6d.
- M'Combie's Cattle and Cattle-Breeders. New Edition, Enlarged, with Memoir of the Author by JAMES MACDONALD. Crown 8vo, 3s. 6d.

MACGREGOR. Life and Opinions of Major-General Sir Charles MacGregor K.C.B., C.S.I., C.I.E., Quartermaster-General of India. From his Letters and Diaries. Edited by Lady MACGREGOR. With Portraits and Maps to illustrate Campaigns in which he was engaged. 2 vols. 8vo, 35s.

M'INTOSH. The Book of the Garden. By CHARLES M'INTOSH, formerly Curator of the Royal Gardens of his Majesty the King of the Belgians, and lately of those of his Grace the Duke of Buccleuch, K.G., at Dalkeith Palace. 2 vols. royal 8vo, with 1350 Engravings. £4, 7s. 6d. Vol. I. On the Formation of Gardens and Construction of Garden Edifices, £2, 10s. Vol. II. Practical Gardening, £1, 17s. 6d.

MACINTYRE. Hindu-Koh: Wanderings and Wild Sports on and beyond the Himalayas. By Major-General DONALD MACINTYRE, V.C., late Prince of Wales' Own Goorkhas, F.R.G.S. Dedicated to H.R.H. The Prince of Wales. New and Cheaper Edition, Revised, with numerous Illustrations. Post 8vo, 7s. 6d.

MACKAY. A Sketch of the History of Fife and Kinross. A Study of Scottish History and Character. By Æ. J. G. MACKAY, Sheriff of these Counties. Crown 8vo, 6s.

MACKAY.
- A Manual of Modern Geography; Mathematical, Physical, and Political. By the Rev. ALEXANDER MACKAY, LL.D., F.R.G.S. 11th Thousand, Revised to the present time. Crown 8vo, pp. 688, 7s. 6d.
- Elements of Modern Geography. 55th Thousand, Revised to the present time. Crown 8vo, pp. 300, 3s.
- The Intermediate Geography. Intended as an Intermediate Book between the Author's 'Outlines of Geography' and 'Elements of Geography.' Seventeenth Edition, Revised. Crown 8vo, pp. 238, 2s.

MACKAY.
  Outlines of Modern Geography. 188th Thousand, Revised to the present time. 18mo, pp. 118, 1s.
  First Steps in Geography. 105th Thousand. 18mo, pp. 56. Sewed, 4d.; cloth, 6d.
  Elements of Physiography and Physical Geography. With Express Reference to the Instructions issued by the Science and Art Department. 30th Thousand, Revised. Crown 8vo, 1s. 6d.
  Facts and Dates; or, The Leading Events in Sacred and Profane History, and the Principal Facts in the various Physical Sciences. For Schools and Private Reference. New Edition. Crown 8vo, 3s. 6d.

MACKAY. An Old Scots Brigade. Being the History of Mackay's Regiment, now incorporated with the Royal Scots. With an Appendix containing many Original Documents connected with the History of the Regiment. By JOHN MACKAY (late) OF HERRIESDALE. Crown 8vo, 5s.

MACKENZIE. Studies in Roman Law. With Comparative Views of the Laws of France, England, and Scotland. By Lord MACKENZIE, one of the Judges of the Court of Session in Scotland. Sixth Edition, Edited by JOHN KIRKPATRICK, M.A., LL.B., Advocate, Professor of History in the University of Edinburgh. 8vo, 12s.

MACPHERSON. Glimpses of Church and Social Life in the Highlands in the Olden Times. By ALEXANDER MACPHERSON, F.S.A. Scot. With Illustrations. In one volume. Small 4to. [*In the press.*

M'PHERSON.
  Summer Sundays in a Strathmore Parish. By J. GORDON M'PHERSON, Ph.D., F.R.S.E., Minister of Ruthven. Crown 8vo, 5s.
  Golf and Golfers. Past and Present. With an Introduction by the Right Hon. A. J. BALFOUR, and a Portrait of the Author. Fcap. 8vo, 1s. 6d.

MACRAE. A Handbook of Deer-Stalking. By ALEXANDER MACRAE, late Forester to Lord Henry Bentinck. With Introduction by Horatio Ross, Esq. Fcap. 8vo, with two Photographs from Life. 3s. 6d.

MAIN. Three Hundred English Sonnets. Chosen and Edited by DAVID M. MAIN. Fcap. 8vo, 6s.

MAIR. A Digest of Laws and Decisions, Ecclesiastical and Civil, relating to the Constitution, Practice, and Affairs of the Church of Scotland. With Notes and Forms of Procedure. By the Rev. WILLIAM MAIR, D.D., Minister of the Parish of Earlston. Crown 8vo. With Supplements. 8s.

MARSHALL.
  French Home Life. By FREDERICK MARSHALL, Author of 'Claire Brandon.' Second Edition. 5s.
  It Happened Yesterday. A Novel. Crown 8vo, 6s.

MARSHMAN. History of India. From the Earliest Period to the Close of the India Company's Government; with an Epitome of Subsequent Events. By JOHN CLARK MARSHMAN, C.S.I. Abridged from the Author's larger work. Second Edition, Revised. Crown 8vo, with Map, 6s. 6d.

MARTIN.
  Goethe's Faust. Part I. Translated by Sir THEODORE MARTIN, K.C.B. Second Edition, crown 8vo, 6s. Ninth Edition, fcap. 8vo, 3s. 6d.
  Goethe's Faust. Part II. Translated into English Verse. Second Edition, Revised. Fcap. 8vo, 6s.
  The Works of Horace. Translated into English Verse, with Life and Notes. 2 vols. New Edition, crown 8vo, 21s.
  Poems and Ballads of Heinrich Heine. Done into English Verse. Second Edition. Printed on papier vergé, crown 8vo, 8s.

MARTIN.
  The Song of the Bell, and other Translations from Schiller, Goethe, Uhland, and Others. Crown 8vo, 7s. 6d.
  Catullus. With Life and Notes. Second Edition, Revised and Corrected. Post 8vo, 7s. 6d.
  Aladdin: A Dramatic Poem. By ADAM OEHLENSCHLAEGER. Fcap. 8vo, 5s.
  Correggio: A Tragedy. By OEHLENSCHLAEGER. With Notes. Fcap. 8vo, 3s.
  King Rene's Daughter: A Danish Lyrical Drama. By HENRIK HERTZ. Second Edition, fcap., 2s. 6d.

MARTIN. On some of Shakespeare's Female Characters. In a Series of Letters. By HELENA FAUCIT, Lady MARTIN. Dedicated by permission to Her Most Gracious Majesty the Queen. New Edition, Enlarged. 8vo, with Portrait by Lane, 7s. 6d. Bound in cloth, gilt edges, 8s. 6d.

MARWICK. Observations on the Law and Practice in regard to Municipal Elections and the Conduct of the Business of Town Councils and Commissioners of Police in Scotland. By Sir JAMES D. MARWICK, LL.D., Town-Clerk of Glasgow. Royal 8vo, 30s.

MATHESON.
  Can the Old Faith Live with the New? or, The Problem of Evolution and Revelation. By the Rev. GEORGE MATHESON, D.D. Third Edition. Crown 8vo, 7s. 6d.
  The Psalmist and the Scientist; or, Modern Value of the Religious Sentiment. New and Cheaper Edition. Crown 8vo, 5s.
  Spiritual Development of St Paul. Third Edition. Cr. 8vo, 5s.
  The Distinctive Messages of the Old Religions. Cr. 8vo, 5s.
  Sacred Songs. New and Cheaper Edition. Crown 8vo, 2s. 6d.

MAURICE. The Balance of Military Power in Europe. An Examination of the War Resources of Great Britain and the Continental States. By Colonel MAURICE, R.A., Professor of Military Art and History at the Royal Staff College. Crown 8vo, with a Map, 6s.

MAXWELL. Meridiana: Noontide Essays. By Sir HERBERT MAXWELL, Bart., M.P., F.S.A., &c., Author of 'Passages in the Life of Sir Lucian Elphin,' &c. Post 8vo, 7s. 6d.

MEREDYTH. The Brief for the Government, 1886-92. A Handbook for Conservative and Unionist Writers, Speakers, &c. Second Edition. By W. H. MEREDYTH. Crown 8vo, 2s. 6d.

MICHEL. A Critical Inquiry into the Scottish Language. With the view of Illustrating the Rise and Progress of Civilisation in Scotland. By FRANCISQUE-MICHEL, F.S.A. Lond. and Scot. Correspondant de l'Institut de France, &c. 4to, printed on hand-made paper, and bound in roxburghe, 66s.

MICHIE.
  The Larch: Being a Practical Treatise on its Culture and General Management. By CHRISTOPHER Y. MICHIE, Forester, Cullen House. Crown 8vo, with Illustrations. New and Cheaper Edition, Enlarged, 5s.
  The Practice of Forestry. Crown 8vo, with Illustrations. 6s.

MIDDLETON. The Story of Alastair Bhan Comyn; or, The Tragedy of Dunphail. A Tale of Tradition and Romance. By the Lady MIDDLETON. Square 8vo, 10s. Cheaper Edition, 5s.

MILLER. Landscape Geology. A Plea for the Study of Geology by Landscape Painters. By HUGH MILLER, of H.M. Geological Survey. Crown 8vo, 3s. Cheap Edition, paper cover, 1s.

MILNE-HOME. Mamma's Black Nurse Stories. West Indian Folk-lore. By MARY PAMELA MILNE-HOME. With six full-page tinted Illustrations. Small 4to, 5s.

MINTO.
A Manual of English Prose Literature, Biographical and Critical: designed mainly to show Characteristics of Style. By W. MINTO, M.A., Professor of Logic in the University of Aberdeen. Third Edition, Revised. Crown 8vo, 7s. 6d.

Characteristics of English Poets, from Chaucer to Shirley. New Edition, Revised. Crown 8vo, 7s. 6d.

MOIR. Life of Mansie Wauch, Tailor in Dalkeith. By D. M. MOIR. With 8 Illustrations on Steel, by the late GEORGE CRUIKSHANK. Crown 8vo, 3s. 6d. Another Edition, fcap. 8vo, 1s. 6d.

MOMERIE.
Defects of Modern Christianity, and other Sermons. By ALFRED WILLIAMS MOMERIE, M.A., D.Sc., LL.D. Fourth Edition. Crown 8vo, 5s.

The Basis of Religion. Being an Examination of Natural Religion. Third Edition. Crown 8vo, 2s. 6d.

The Origin of Evil, and other Sermons. Seventh Edition, Enlarged. Crown 8vo, 5s.

Personality. The Beginning and End of Metaphysics, and a Necessary Assumption in all Positive Philosophy. Fourth Edition, Revised. Crown 8vo, 3s.

Agnosticism. Fourth Edition, Revised. Crown 8vo, 5s.

Preaching and Hearing; and other Sermons. Third Edition, Enlarged. Crown 8vo, 5s.

Belief in God. Third Edition. Crown 8vo, 3s.

Inspiration; and other Sermons. Second Edition, Enlarged. Crown 8vo, 5s.

Church and Creed. Second Edition. Crown 8vo, 4s. 6d.

MONTAGUE. Campaigning in South Africa. Reminiscences of an Officer in 1879. By Captain W. E. MONTAGUE, 94th Regiment, Author of 'Claude Meadowleigh,' &c. 8vo, 10s. 6d.

MONTALEMBERT. Memoir of Count de Montalembert. A Chapter of Recent French History. By Mrs OLIPHANT, Author of the 'Life of Edward Irving,' &c. 2 vols. crown 8vo, £1, 4s.

MORISON.
Æolus. A Romance in Lyrics. By JEANIE MORISON. Crown 8vo, 3s.

There as Here. Crown 8vo, 3s.
 *** A limited impression on hand-made paper, bound in vellum, 7s. 6d.

Selections from Poems. Crown 8vo, 4s. 6d.

Sordello. An Outline Analysis of Mr Browning's Poem. Crown 8vo, 3s.

Of "Fifine at the Fair," "Christmas Eve and Easter Day," and other of Mr Browning's Poems. Crown 8vo, 3s.

The Purpose of the Ages. Crown 8vo, 9s.

Gordon: An Our-day Idyll. Crown 8vo, 3s.

Saint Isadora, and other Poems. Crown 8vo, 1s. 6d.

Snatches of Song. Paper, 1s. 6d.; Cloth, 3s.

MORISON.
    Pontius Pilate. Paper, 1s. 6d. ; Cloth, 3s.
    Mill o' Forres. Crown 8vo, 1s.
    Ane Booke of Ballades. Fcap. 4to, 1s.

MOZLEY. Essays from 'Blackwood.' By the late ANNE MOZLEY, Author of 'Essays on Social Subjects'; Editor of 'The Letters and Correspondence of Cardinal Newman,' 'Letters of the Rev. J. B. Mozley,' &c. With a Memoir by her Sister, FANNY MOZLEY. Post 8vo, 7s. 6d.

MUNRO. On Valuation of Property. By WILLIAM MUNRO, M.A., Her Majesty's Assessor of Railways and Canals for Scotland. Second Edition, Revised and Enlarged. 8vo, 3s. 6d.

MURDOCH. Manual of the Law of Insolvency and Bankruptcy: Comprehending a Summary of the Law of Insolvency, Notour Bankruptcy, Composition-contracts, Trust-deeds, Cessios, and Sequestrations; and the Winding-up of Joint-Stock Companies in Scotland; with Annotations on the various Insolvency and Bankruptcy Statutes; and with Forms of Procedure applicable to these Subjects. By JAMES MURDOCH, Member of the Faculty of Procurators in Glasgow. Fifth Edition, Revised and Enlarged. 8vo, £1, 10s.

MY TRIVIAL LIFE AND MISFORTUNE: A Gossip with no Plot in Particular. By A PLAIN WOMAN. Cheap Edition. Crown 8vo, 3s. 6d.

    By the SAME AUTHOR.
    POOR NELLIE. Cheap Edition. Crown 8vo, 3s. 6d.

NAPIER. The Construction of the Wonderful Canon of Logarithms. By JOHN NAPIER of Merchiston. Translated, with Notes, and a Catalogue of Napier's Works, by WILLIAM RAE MACDONALD. Small 4to, 15s. *A few large-paper copies on Whatman paper, 30s.*

NEAVES.
    Songs and Verses, Social and Scientific. By An Old Contributor to 'Maga.' By the Hon. Lord NEAVES. Fifth Edition. Fcap. 8vo, 4s.
    The Greek Anthology. Being Vol. XX. of 'Ancient Classics for English Readers.' Crown 8vo, 2s. 6d.

NICHOLSON.
    A Manual of Zoology, for the use of Students. With a General Introduction on the Principles of Zoology. By HENRY ALLEYNE NICHOLSON, M.D., D.Sc., F.L.S., F.G.S., Regius Professor of Natural History in the University of Aberdeen. Seventh Edition, Rewritten and Enlarged. Post 8vo, pp. 956, with 555 Engravings on Wood, 18s.

    Text-Book of Zoology, for the use of Schools. Fourth Edition, Enlarged. Crown 8vo, with 188 Engravings on Wood, 7s. 6d.

    Introductory Text-Book of Zoology, for the use of Junior Classes. Sixth Edition, Revised and Enlarged, with 166 Engravings, 3s.

    Outlines of Natural History, for Beginners: being Descriptions of a Progressive Series of Zoological Types. Third Edition, with Engravings, 1s. 6d.

    A Manual of Palæontology, for the use of Students. With a General Introduction on the Principles of Palæontology. By Professor H. ALLEYNE NICHOLSON and RICHARD LYDEKKER, B.A. Third Edition, entirely Rewritten and greatly Enlarged. 2 vols. 8vo, £3, 3s.

    The Ancient Life-History of the Earth. An Outline of the Principles and Leading Facts of Palæontological Science. Crown 8vo, with 276 Engravings, 10s. 6d.

    On the "Tabulate Corals" of the Palæozoic Period, with Critical Descriptions of Illustrative Species. Illustrated with 15 Lithographed Plates and numerous Engravings. Super-royal 8vo, 21s.

NICHOLSON.
Synopsis of the Classification of the Animal Kingdom. 8vo, with 106 Illustrations, 6s.

On the Structure and Affinities of the Genus Monticulipora and its Sub-Genera, with Critical Descriptions of Illustrative Species. Illustrated with numerous Engravings on Wood and Lithographed Plates. Super-royal 8vo, 18s.

NICHOLSON.
Communion with Heaven, and other Sermons. By the late MAXWELL NICHOLSON, D.D., Minister of St Stephen's, Edinburgh. Crown 8vo, 5s. 6d.

Rest in Jesus. Sixth Edition. Fcap. 8vo, 4s. 6d.

NICHOLSON.
A Treatise on Money, and Essays on Present Monetary Problems. By JOSEPH SHIELD NICHOLSON, M.A., D.Sc., Professor of Commercial and Political Economy and Mercantile Law in the University of Edinburgh. 8vo, 10s. 6d.

Thoth. A Romance. Third Edition. Crown 8vo, 4s. 6d.

A Dreamer of Dreams. A Modern Romance. Second Edition. Crown 8vo, 6s.

NICOLSON AND MURE.
A Handbook to the Local Government (Scotland) Act, 1889. With Introduction, Explanatory Notes, and Index. By J. BADENACH NICOLSON, Advocate, Counsel to the Scotch Education Department, and W. J. MURE, Advocate, Legal Secretary to the Lord Advocate for Scotland. Ninth Reprint. 8vo, 5s.

OLIPHANT.
Masollam: A Problem of the Period. A Novel. By LAURENCE OLIPHANT. 3 vols. post 8vo, 25s. 6d.

Scientific Religion; or, Higher Possibilities of Life and Practice through the Operation of Natural Forces. Second Edition. 8vo, 16s.

Altiora Peto. Cheap Edition. Crown 8vo, boards, 2s. 6d.; cloth, 3s. 6d. Illustrated Edition. Crown 8vo, cloth, 6s.

Piccadilly. With Illustrations by Richard Doyle. New Edition, 3s. 6d. Cheap Edition, boards, 2s. 6d.

Traits and Travesties; Social and Political. Post 8vo, 10s. 6d.

Episodes in a Life of Adventure; or, Moss from a Rolling Stone. Fifth Edition. Post 8vo, 6s.

Haifa: Life in Modern Palestine. Second Edition. 8vo, 7s. 6d.

The Land of Gilead. With Excursions in the Lebanon. With Illustrations and Maps. Demy 8vo, 21s.

Memoir of the Life of Laurence Oliphant, and of Alice Oliphant, his Wife. By Mrs M. O. W. OLIPHANT. Seventh Edition. 2 vols. post 8vo, with Portraits. 21s.
POPULAR EDITION. With a New Preface. Post 8vo, with Portraits. 7s. 6d.

OLIPHANT.
Katie Stewart. By Mrs OLIPHANT. Illustrated boards, 2s. 6d.

Katie Stewart, and other Stories. New Edition. Crown 8vo, cloth, 3s. 6d.

Valentine and his Brother. New Edition. Crown 8vo, 3s. 6d.

Sons and Daughters. Crown 8vo, 3s. 6d.

OLIPHANT.
  Diana Trelawny: The History of a Great Mistake. 2 vols. crown 8vo, 17s.
  Two Stories of the Seen and the Unseen. The Open Door —Old Lady Mary. Paper covers, 1s.

OLIPHANT. Notes of a Pilgrimage to Jerusalem and the Holy Land. By F. R. OLIPHANT. Crown 8vo, 3s. 6d.

ON SURREY HILLS. By "A SON OF THE MARSHES." *See page 28.*

OSSIAN. The Poems of Ossian in the Original Gaelic. With a Literal Translation into English, and a Dissertation on the Authenticity of the Poems. By the Rev. ARCHIBALD CLERK. 2 vols. imperial 8vo, £1, 11s. 6d.

OSWALD. By Fell and Fjord; or, Scenes and Studies in Iceland. By E. J. OSWALD. Post 8vo, with Illustrations. 7s. 6d.

PAGE.
  Introductory Text-Book of Geology. By DAVID PAGE, LL.D., Professor of Geology in the Durham University of Physical Science, Newcastle, and Professor LAPWORTH of Mason Science College, Birmingham. With Engravings and Glossarial Index. Twelfth Edition, Revised and Enlarged. 3s. 6d.
  Advanced Text-Book of Geology, Descriptive and Industrial. With Engravings, and Glossary of Scientific Terms. Sixth Edition, Revised and Enlarged. 7s. 6d.
  Introductory Text-Book of Physical Geography. With Sketch-Maps and Illustrations. Edited by Professor LAPWORTH, LL.D., F.G.S., &c., Mason Science College, Birmingham. Twelfth Edition, Revised. 2s. 6d.
  Advanced Text-Book of Physical Geography. Third Edition, Revised and Enlarged by Professor LAPWORTH. With Engravings. 5s.

PATON.
  Spindrift. By Sir J. NOEL PATON. Fcap., cloth, 5s.
  Poems by a Painter. Fcap., cloth, 5s.

PATON. Body and Soul. A Romance in Transcendental Pathology. By FREDERICK NOEL PATON. Third Edition. Crown 8vo, 1s.

PATRICK. The Apology of Origen in Reply to Celsus. A Chapter in the History of Apologetics. By the Rev. J. PATRICK, B.D. Post 8vo, 7s. 6d.

PATTERSON.
  Essays in History and Art. By R. HOGARTH PATTERSON. 8vo, 12s.
  The New Golden Age, and Influence of the Precious Metals upon the World. 2 vols. 8vo, 31s. 6d.

PAUL. History of the Royal Company of Archers, the Queen's Body-Guard for Scotland. By JAMES BALFOUR PAUL, Advocate of the Scottish Bar. Crown 4to, with Portraits and other Illustrations. £2, 2s.

PEILE. Lawn Tennis as a Game of Skill. With latest revised Laws as played by the Best Clubs. By Captain S. C. F. PEILE, B.S.C. Cheaper Edition. Fcap., cloth, 1s.

PETTIGREW. The Handy Book of Bees, and their Profitable Management. By A. PETTIGREW. Fifth Edition, Enlarged, with Engravings. Crown 8vo, 3s. 6d.

PHILIP. The Function of Labour in the Production of Wealth. By ALEXANDER PHILIP, LL.B., Edinburgh. Crown 8vo, 3s. 6d.

PHILOSOPHICAL CLASSICS FOR ENGLISH READERS. Edited by WILLIAM KNIGHT, LL.D., Professor of Moral Philosophy, University of St Andrews. In crown 8vo volumes, with Portraits, price 3s. 6d.
[*For list of Volumes published, see page 2.*]

POLLOK. The Course of Time: A Poem. By ROBERT POLLOK, A.M. Cottage Edition, 32mo, 8d. The Same, cloth, gilt edges, 1s. 6d. Another Edition, with Illustrations by Birket Foster and others, fcap., cloth, 3s. 6d., or with edges gilt, 4s.

PORT ROYAL LOGIC. Translated from the French; with Introduction, Notes, and Appendix. By THOMAS SPENCER BAYNES, LL.D., Professor in the University of St Andrews. Tenth Edition, 12mo, 4s.

POTTS AND DARNELL.
Aditus Faciliores: An Easy Latin Construing Book, with Complete Vocabulary. By A. W. POTTS, M.A., LL.D., and the Rev. C. DARNELL, M.A., Head-Master of Cargilfield Preparatory School, Edinburgh. Tenth Edition, fcap. 8vo, 3s. 6d.

Aditus Faciliores Graeci. An Easy Greek Construing Book, with Complete Vocabulary. Fifth Edition, Revised. Fcap. 8vo, 3s.

POTTS. School Sermons. By the late ALEXANDER WM. POTTS, LL.D., First Head-Master of Fettes College. With a Memoir and Portrait. Crown 8vo, 7s. 6d.

PRINGLE. The Live-Stock of the Farm. By ROBERT O. PRINGLE. Third Edition. Revised and Edited by JAMES MACDONALD. Crown 8vo, 7s. 6d.

PUBLIC GENERAL STATUTES AFFECTING SCOTLAND from 1707 to 1847, with Chronological Table and Index. 3 vols. large 8vo, £3, 3s.

PUBLIC GENERAL STATUTES AFFECTING SCOTLAND, COLLECTION OF. Published Annually, with General Index.

RADICAL CURE FOR IRELAND, The. A Letter to the People of England and Scotland concerning a new Plantation. With 2 Maps. 8vo, 7s. 6d.

RAE. The Syrian Church in India. By GEORGE MILNE RAE, M.A., Fellow of the University of Madras; late Professor in the Madras Christian College. With 6 full-page Illustrations. Post 8vo, 10s. 6d.

RAMSAY. Scotland and Scotsmen in the Eighteenth Century. Edited from the MSS. of JOHN RAMSAY, Esq. of Ochtertyre, by ALEXANDER ALLARDYCE, Author of 'Memoir of Admiral Lord Keith, K.B.,' &c. 2 vols. 8vo, 31s. 6d.

RANKIN.
A Handbook of the Church of Scotland. By JAMES RANKIN, D.D., Minister of Muthill; Author of 'Character Studies in the Old Testament,' &c. An entirely New and much Enlarged Edition. Crown 8vo, with 2 Maps, 7s. 6d.

The Creed in Scotland. An Exposition of the Apostles' Creed. With Extracts from Archbishop Hamilton's Catechism of 1552, John Calvin's Catechism of 1556, and a Catena of Ancient Latin and other Hymns. Post 8vo, 7s. 6d.

The Worthy Communicant. A Guide to the Devout Observance of the Lord's Supper. Limp cloth, 1s. 3d.

The Young Churchman. Lessons on the Creed, the Commandments, the Means of Grace, and the Church. Limp cloth, 1s. 3d.

First Communion Lessons. 23d Edition. Paper Cover, 2d.

RECORDS OF **THE TERCENTENARY FESTIVAL OF THE** UNIVERSITY OF EDINBURGH. Celebrated in April 1884. Published under the Sanction of the Senatus Academicus. Large 4to, £2, 12s. 6d.

ROBERTSON. The Early Religion of Israel. As set forth by Biblical Writers and Modern Critical Historians. Being the Baird Lecture for 1888-89. By JAMES ROBERTSON, D.D., Professor of Oriental Languages in the University of Glasgow. Third Edition. Crown 8vo, 10s. 6d.

ROBERTSON. Orellana, and other Poems. By J. LOGIE ROBERTSON, M.A. Fcap. 8vo. Printed on hand-made paper. 6s.

ROBERTSON. Our Holiday among the Hills. By JAMES and JANET LOGIE ROBERTSON. Fcap. 8vo, 3s. 6d.

ROBERTSON. Essays and Sermons. By the late W. ROBERTSON, B.D., Minister of the Parish of Sprouston. With a Memoir and Portrait. Crown 8vo, 5s. 6d.

RODGER. Aberdeen Doctors at Home and Abroad. The Story of a Medical School. By ELLA HILL BURTON RODGER. In one volume, demy 8vo. [*In the press.*

ROSCOE. Rambles with a Fishing-rod. By E. S. ROSCOE. Crown 8vo, 4s. 6d.

ROSS. Old Scottish Regimental Colours. By ANDREW ROSS, S.S.C., Hon. Secretary Old Scottish Regimental Colours Committee. Dedicated by Special Permission to Her Majesty the Queen. Folio. £2, 12s. 6d.

RUSSELL. The Haigs of Bemersyde. A Family History. By JOHN RUSSELL. Large 8vo, with Illustrations. 21s.

RUSSELL. Fragments from Many Tables. Being the Recollections of some Wise and Witty Men and Women. By GEORGE RUSSELL. Crown 8vo, 4s. 6d.

RUTLAND.
Notes of an Irish Tour in 1846. By the DUKE OF RUTLAND, G.C.B. (Lord JOHN MANNERS). New Edition. Crown 8vo, 2s. 6d.
Correspondence between the Right Honble. William Pitt and Charles Duke of Rutland, Lord-Lieutenant of Ireland, 1781-1787. With Introductory Note by JOHN DUKE OF RUTLAND. 8vo, 7s. 6d.

RUTLAND.
Gems of German Poetry. Translated by the DUCHESS OF RUTLAND (Lady JOHN MANNERS). [*New Edition in preparation.*
Impressions of Bad-Homburg. Comprising a Short Account of the Women's Associations of Germany under the Red Cross. Crown 8vo, 1s. 6d.
Some Personal Recollections of the Later Years of the Earl of Beaconsfield, K.G. Sixth Edition, 6d.
Employment of Women in the Public Service. 6d.
Some of the Advantages of Easily Accessible Reading and Recreation Rooms, and Free Libraries. With Remarks on Starting and Maintaining them. Second Edition. Crown 8vo, 1s.
A Sequel to Rich Men's Dwellings, and other Occasional Papers. Crown 8vo, 2s. 6d.
Encouraging Experiences of Reading and Recreation Rooms, Aims of Guilds, Nottingham Social Guide, Existing Institutions, &c., &c. Crown 8vo, 1s.

SCHILLER. Wallenstein. A Dramatic Poem. By FRIEDRICH VON SCHILLER. Translated by C. G. N. LOCKHART. Fcap. 8vo, 7s. 6d.

SCOTCH LOCH FISHING. By "BLACK PALMER." Crown 8vo, Interleaved with blank pages, 4s.

SCOUGAL. Prisons and their Inmates; or, Scenes from a Silent World. By FRANCIS SCOUGAL. Crown 8vo, boards, 2s.

SELLAR. Manual of the Education Acts for Scotland. By the late ALEXANDER CRAIG SELLAR, M.P. Eighth Edition. Revised and in great part rewritten by J. EDWARD GRAHAM, B.A. Oxon., Advocate. With Rules for the conduct of Elections, with Notes and Cases. 8vo.
[*New Edition in preparation.*]
[SUPPLEMENT TO SELLAR'S MANUAL. Being the Acts of 1889 in so far as affecting the Education Acts. 8vo, 2s.]

SETH.
Scottish Philosophy. A Comparison of the Scottish and German Answers to Hume. Balfour Philosophical Lectures, University of Edinburgh. By ANDREW SETH, M.A., Professor of Logic and Metaphysics in Edinburgh University. Second Edition. Crown 8vo, 5s.

Hegelianism and Personality. Balfour Philosophical Lectures. Second Series. Crown 8vo, 5s.

SETH. Freedom as Ethical Postulate. By JAMES SETH, M.A., Brown University, Providence, Rhode Island. 8vo, 1s.

SHADWELL. The Life of Colin Campbell, Lord Clyde. Illustrated by Extracts from his Diary and Correspondence. By Lieutenant-General SHADWELL, C.B. With Portrait, Maps, and Plans. 2 vols. 8vo. 36s.

SHAND.
Half a Century; or, Changes in Men and Manners. By ALEX. INNES SHAND, Author of 'Against Time,' &c. Second Edition. 8vo, 12s. 6d.

Letters from the West of Ireland. Reprinted from the 'Times.' Crown 8vo, 5s.

Kilcarra. A Novel. 3 vols. crown 8vo, 25s. 6d.

SHARPE. Letters from and to Charles Kirkpatrick Sharpe. Edited by ALEXANDER ALLARDYCE, Author of 'Memoir of Admiral Lord Keith, K.B.,' &c. With a Memoir by the Rev. W. K. R. BEDFORD. In 2 vols. 8vo. Illustrated with Etchings and other Engravings. £2, 12s. 6d.

SIM. Margaret Sim's Cookery. With an Introduction by L. B. WALFORD, Author of 'Mr Smith: A Part of his Life,' &c. Crown 8vo, 5s.

SKELTON.
Maitland of Lethington; and the Scotland of Mary Stuart. A History. By JOHN SKELTON, C.B., LL.D., Author of 'The Essays of Shirley.' Demy 8vo, 2 vols., 28s.

The Handbook of Public Health. A Complete Edition of the Public Health and other Sanitary Acts relating to Scotland. Annotated, and with the Rules, Instructions, and Decisions of the Board of Supervision brought up to date with relative forms. Second Edition. With Introduction, containing the Administration of the Public Health Act in Counties. 8vo, 8s. 6d.

The Local Government (Scotland) Act in Relation to Public Health. A Handy Guide for County and District Councillors, Medical Officers, Sanitary Inspectors, and Members of Parochial Boards. Second Edition. With a new Preface on appointment of Sanitary Officers. Crown 8vo, 2s.

SKRINE. Columba: A Drama. By JOHN HUNTLEY SKRINE, Warden of Glenalmond; Author of 'A Memory of Edward Thring.' Fcap. 4to.
[*Immediately.*]

SMITH. For God and Humanity. A Romance of Mount Carmel. By HASKETT SMITH, Author of 'The Divine Epiphany,' &c. 3 vols. post 8vo, 25s. 6d.

SMITH.
: Thorndale; or, The Conflict of Opinions. By WILLIAM SMITH, Author of 'A Discourse on Ethics,' &c. New Edition. Crown 8vo, 10s. 6d.
: Gravenhurst; or, Thoughts on Good and Evil. Second Edition. With Memoir and Portrait of the Author. Crown 8vo, 8s.
: The Story of William and Lucy Smith. Edited by GEORGE MERRIAM. Large post 8vo, 12s. 6d.

SMITH. Memoir of the Families of M'Combie and Thoms, originally M'Intosh and M'Thomas. Compiled from History and Tradition. By WILLIAM M'COMBIE SMITH. With Illustrations. 8vo, 7s. 6d.

SMITH. Greek Testament Lessons for Colleges, Schools, and Private Students, consisting chiefly of the Sermon on the Mount and the Parables of our Lord. With Notes and Essays. By the Rev. J. HUNTER SMITH, M.A., King Edward's School, Birmingham. Crown 8vo, 6s.

SMITH. Writings by the Way. By JOHN CAMPBELL SMITH, M.A., Sheriff-Substitute. Crown 8vo, 9s.

SMITH. The Secretary for Scotland. Being a Statement of the Powers and Duties of the new Scottish Office. With a Short Historical Introduction and numerous references to important Administrative Documents. By W. C. SMITH, LL.B., Advocate. 8vo, 6s.

"SON OF THE MARSHES, A."
: Within an Hour of London Town: Among Wild Birds and their Haunts. By "A SON OF THE MARSHES." Edited by J. A. OWEN. Second Edition. Crown 8vo, 6s.
: On Surrey Hills. Third Edition. Crown 8vo, 6s.
: Annals of a Fishing Village. New and Cheaper Edition. Crown 8vo, 5s. Illustrated Edition. Crown 8vo, 7s. 6d.

SORLEY. The Ethics of Naturalism. Being the Shaw Fellowship Lectures, 1884. By W. R. SORLEY, M.A., Fellow of Trinity College, Cambridge, Professor of Logic and Philosophy in University College of South Wales. Crown 8vo, 6s.

SPEEDY. Sport in the Highlands and Lowlands of Scotland with Rod and Gun. By TOM SPEEDY. Second Edition, Revised and Enlarged. With Illustrations by Lieut.-General Hope Crealocke, C.B., C.M.G., and others. 8vo, 15s.

SPROTT. The Worship and Offices of the Church of Scotland. By GEORGE W. SPROTT, D.D., Minister of North Berwick. Crown 8vo, 6s.

STARFORTH. Villa Residences and Farm Architecture: A Series of Designs. By JOHN STARFORTH, Architect. 102 Engravings. Second Edition. Medium 4to, £2, 17s. 6d.

STATISTICAL ACCOUNT OF SCOTLAND. Complete, with Index. 15 vols. 8vo, £16, 16s.

STEPHENS.
: Book of the Farm; detailing the Labours of the Farmer, Farm-Steward, Ploughman, Shepherd, Hedger, Farm-Labourer, Field-Worker, and Cattle-man. Illustrated with numerous Portraits of Animals and Engravings of Implements, and Plans of Farm Buildings. Fourth Edition. Revised, and in great part Rewritten by JAMES MACDONALD, of the 'Farming World,' &c. Complete in Six Divisional Volumes, bound in cloth, each 10s. 6d., or handsomely bound, in 3 volumes, with leather back and gilt top, £3, 3s.
: The Book of Farm Implements and Machines. By J. SLIGHT and R. SCOTT BURN, Engineers. Edited by HENRY STEPHENS. Large 8vo, £2, 2s.
: Catechism of Agriculture. [*New Edition in preparation.*

STEVENSON. British Fungi. (Hymenomycetes). By Rev. JOHN STEVENSON, Author of 'Mycologia Scotia,' Hon. Sec. Cryptogamic Society of Scotland. Vols. I. and II., post 8vo, with Illustrations, price 12s. 6d. net each.

STEWART.
Advice to Purchasers of Horses. By JOHN STEWART, V.S. New Edition. 2s. 6d.

Stable Economy. A Treatise on the Management of Horses in relation to Stabling, Grooming, Feeding, Watering, and Working. Seventh Edition. Fcap. 8vo, 6s. 6d.

STEWART. A Hebrew Grammar, with the Pronunciation, Syllabic Division and Tone of the Words, and Quantity of the Vowels. By Rev. DUNCAN STEWART, D.D. Fourth Edition. 8vo, 3s. 6d.

STEWART. Boethius: An Essay. By HUGH FRASER STEWART, M.A., Trinity College, Cambridge. Crown 8vo, 7s. 6d.

STODDART. Angling Songs. By THOMAS TOD STODDART. New Edition, with a Memoir by ANNA M. STODDART. Crown 8vo, 7s. 6d.

STORMONTH.
Etymological and Pronouncing Dictionary of the English Language. Including a very Copious Selection of Scientific Terms. For use in Schools and Colleges, and as a Book of General Reference. By the Rev. JAMES STORMONTH. The Pronunciation carefully revised by the Rev. P. H. PHELP, M.A. Cantab. Eleventh Edition, Revised throughout, with Supplement. Crown 8vo, pp. 800. 7s. 6d.

Dictionary of the English Language, Pronouncing, Etymological, and Explanatory. Revised by the Rev. P. H. PHELP. Library Edition. Imperial 8vo, handsomely bound in half morocco, 31s. 6d.

The School Etymological Dictionary and Word-Book. Fourth Edition. Fcap. 8vo, pp. 254. 2s.

STORY.
Nero; A Historical Play. By W. W. STORY, Author of 'Roba di Roma.' Fcap. 8vo, 6s.

Vallombrosa. Post 8vo, 5s.

Poems. 2 vols., 7s. 6d.

Fiammetta. A Summer Idyl. Crown 8vo, 7s. 6d.

Conversations in a Studio. 2 vols. crown 8vo, 12s. 6d.

Excursions in Art and Letters. Crown 8vo, 7s. 6d.

STRICKLAND. Life of Agnes Strickland. By her SISTER. Post 8vo, with Portrait engraved on Steel, 12s. 6d.

STURGIS.
John-a-Dreams. A Tale. By JULIAN STURGIS. New Edition. Crown 8vo, 3s. 6d.

Little Comedies, Old and New. Crown 8vo, 7s. 6d.

SUTHERLAND (DUCHESS OF). How I Spent my Twentieth Year. Being a Record of a Tour Round the World, 1886-7. By the Duchess OF SUTHERLAND (MARCHIONESS OF STAFFORD). With Illustrations. Crown 8vo, 7s. 6d.

SUTHERLAND. Handbook of Hardy Herbaceous and Alpine Flowers, for General Garden Decoration. Containing Descriptions of upwards of 1000 Species of Ornamental Hardy Perennial and Alpine Plants; along with Concise and Plain Instructions for their Propagation and Culture. By WILLIAM SUTHERLAND, Landscape Gardener; formerly Manager of the Herbaceous Department at Kew. Crown 8vo, 7s. 6d.

TAYLOR. The Story of my Life. By the late Colonel MEADOWS TAYLOR, Author of 'The Confessions of a Thug,' &c., &c. Edited by his Daughter. New and Cheaper Edition, being the Fourth. Crown 8vo, 6s.

THOLUCK. Hours of Christian Devotion. Translated from the German of A. Tholuck, D.D., Professor of Theology in the University of Halle. By the Rev. ROBERT MENZIES, D.D. With a Preface written for this Translation by the Author. Second Edition. Crown 8vo, 7s. 6d.

THOMSON. A History of the Fife Light Horse. By Colonel ANSTRUTHER THOMSON. With numerous Portraits. Small 4to. 21s.

THOMSON.

Handy Book of the Flower-Garden: being Practical Directions for the Propagation, Culture, and Arrangement of Plants in Flower-Gardens all the year round. With Engraved Plans. By DAVID THOMSON, Gardener to his Grace the Duke of Buccleuch, K.T., at Drumlanrig. Fourth and Cheaper Edition. Crown 8vo, 5s.

The Handy Book of Fruit-Culture under Glass: being a series of Elaborate Practical Treatises on the Cultivation and Forcing of Pines, Vines, Peaches, Figs, Melons, Strawberries, and Cucumbers. With Engravings of Hothouses, &c. Second Edition, Revised and Enlarged. Crown 8vo, 7s. 6d.

THOMSON. A Practical Treatise on the Cultivation of the Grape Vine. By WILLIAM THOMSON, Tweed Vineyards. Tenth Edition. 8vo, 5s.

THOMSON. Cookery for the Sick and Convalescent. With Directions for the Preparation of Poultices, Fomentations, &c. By BARBARA THOMSON. Fcap. 8vo, 1s. 6d.

THORNTON. Opposites. A Series of Essays on the Unpopular Sides of Popular Questions. By LEWIS THORNTON. 8vo, 12s. 6d.

TOM CRINGLE'S LOG. A New Edition, with Illustrations. Crown 8vo, cloth gilt, 5s. Cheap Edition, 2s.

TRANSACTIONS OF THE HIGHLAND AND AGRICULTURAL SOCIETY OF SCOTLAND. Published annually, price 5s.

TRAVEL, ADVENTURE, AND SPORT. From 'Blackwood's Magazine.' Uniform with 'Tales from Blackwood.' In 12 Parts, each price 1s. Handsomely bound in 6 vols., cloth, 15s.; half calf, 25s.

TRAVERS. Mona Maclean, Medical Student. A Novel. By GRAHAM TRAVERS. 3 vols. crown 8vo, 25s. 6d.

TULLOCH.

Rational Theology and Christian Philosophy in England in the Seventeenth Century. By JOHN TULLOCH, D.D., Principal of St Mary's College in the University of St Andrews; and one of her Majesty's Chaplains in Ordinary in Scotland. Second Edition. 2 vols. 8vo, 16s.

Modern Theories in Philosophy and Religion. 8vo, 15s.

Luther, and other Leaders of the Reformation. Third Edition, Enlarged. Crown 8vo, 3s. 6d.

Memoir of Principal Tulloch, D.D., LL.D. By Mrs OLIPHANT, Author of 'Life of Edward Irving.' Third and Cheaper Edition. 8vo, with Portrait, 7s. 6d.

TURNBULL. Othello: A Critical Study. By W. R. TURNBULL. Demy 8vo, 15s.

TWEEDIE. The Arabian Horse: his Country and People. With Portraits of Typical or Famous Arabians, and numerous other Illustrations; also a Map of the Country of the Arabian Horse, and a descriptive Glossary of Arabic words and proper names. By Colonel W. TWEEDIE, C.S.I., Bengal Staff Corps, H.B.M.'s Consul-General, Baghdad, and Political Resident for the Government of India in Turkish Arabia. [*In the press.*

VEITCH.
Institutes of Logic. By JOHN VEITCH, LL.D., Professor of Logic and Rhetoric in the University of Glasgow. Post 8vo, 12s. 6d.

History and Poetry of the Scottish Border. In One Volume. Demy 8vo. [*In the press.*

The Feeling for Nature in Scottish Poetry. From the Earliest Times to the Present Day. 2 vols. fcap. 8vo, in roxburghe binding, 15s.

Merlin and other Poems. Fcap. 8vo. 4s. 6d.

Knowing and Being. Essays in Philosophy. First Series. Crown 8vo, 5s.

VIRGIL. The Æneid of Virgil. Translated in English Blank Verse by G. K. RICKARDS, M.A., and Lord RAVENSWORTH. 2 vols. fcap. 8vo, 10s.

WACE. The Christian Faith and Recent Agnostic Attacks. By the Rev. HENRY WACE, D.D., Principal of King's College, London; Preacher of Lincoln's Inn; Chaplain to the Queen. In one vol. post 8vo. [*Shortly.*

WALFORD. Four Biographies from 'Blackwood': Jane Taylor, Hannah More, Elizabeth Fry, Mary Somerville. By L. B. WALFORD. Crown 8vo, 5s.

WARREN'S (SAMUEL) WORKS :—
Diary of a Late Physician. Cloth, 2s. 6d.; boards, 2s.

Ten Thousand A-Year. Cloth, 3s. 6d.; boards, 2s. 6d.

Now and Then. The Lily and the Bee. Intellectual and Moral Development of the Present Age. 4s. 6d.

Essays: Critical, Imaginative, and Juridical. 5s.

WARREN. The Five Books of the Psalms. With Marginal Notes. By Rev. SAMUEL L. WARREN, Rector of Esher, Surrey; late Fellow, Dean, and Divinity Lecturer, Wadham College, Oxford. Crown 8vo, 5s.

WEBSTER. The Angler and the Loop-Rod. By DAVID WEBSTER. Crown 8vo, with Illustrations, 7s. 6d.

WELLINGTON. Wellington Prize Essays on "the System of Field Manœuvres best adapted for enabling our Troops to meet a Continental Army." Edited by General Sir EDWARD BRUCE HAMLEY, K.C.B., K.C.M.G. 8vo, 12s. 6d.

WENLEY. Socrates and Christ: A Study in the Philosophy of Religion. By R. M. WENLEY, M.A., Lecturer on Mental and Moral Philosophy in Queen Margaret College, Glasgow; Examiner in Philosophy in the University of Glasgow. Crown 8vo, 6s.

WERNER. A Visit to Stanley's Rear-Guard at Major Barttelot's Camp on the Aruhwimi. With an Account of River-Life on the Congo. By J. R. WERNER, F.R.G.S., Engineer, late in the Service of the Etat Independant du Congo. With Maps, Portraits, and other Illustrations. 8vo, 16s.

WESTMINSTER ASSEMBLY. Minutes of the Westminster Assembly, while engaged in preparing their Directory for Church Government, Confession of Faith, and Catechisms (November 1644 to March 1649). Edited by the Rev. Professor ALEX. T. MITCHELL, of St Andrews, and the Rev. JOHN STRUTHERS, LL.D. With a Historical and Critical Introduction by Professor Mitchell. 8vo, 15s.

WHITE.
The Eighteen Christian Centuries. By the REV. JAMES WHITE. Seventh Edition, post 8vo, with Index, 6s.

History of France, from the Earliest Times. Sixth Thousand. Post 8vo, with Index, 6s.

WHITE.

Archæological Sketches in Scotland—Kintyre and Knapdale.
By Colonel T. P. WHITE, R.E., of the Ordnance Survey. With numerous Illustrations. 2 vols. folio, £4, 4s. Vol. I., Kintyre, sold separately, £2, 2s.

The Ordnance Survey of the United Kingdom. A Popular Account. Crown 8vo, 5s.

WILLIAMSON. The Horticultural Exhibitor's Handbook. A Treatise on Cultivating, Exhibiting, and Judging Plants, Flowers, Fruits, and Vegetables. By W. WILLIAMSON, Gardener. Revised by MALCOLM DUNN, Gardener to his Grace the Duke of Buccleuch and Queensberry, Dalkeith Park. Crown 8vo, 3s. 6d.

WILLIAMSON. Poems of Nature and Life. By DAVID R. WILLIAMSON, Minister of Kirkmaiden. Fcap. 8vo, 3s.

WILLIAMSON. Light from Eastern Lands on the Lives of Abraham, Joseph, and Moses. By the Rev. ALEX. WILLIAMSON, Author of 'The Missionary Heroes of the Pacific,' 'Sure and Comfortable Words,' 'Ask and Receive,' &c. Crown 8vo, 3s. 6d.

WILLS AND GREENE. Drawing-room Dramas for Children. By W. G. WILLS and the Hon. Mrs GREENE. Crown 8vo, 6s.

WILSON.

Works of Professor Wilson. Edited by his Son-in-Law, Professor FERRIER. 12 vols. crown 8vo, £2, 8s.

Christopher in his Sporting-Jacket. 2 vols., 8s.

Isle of Palms, City of the Plague, and other Poems. 4s.

Lights and Shadows of Scottish Life, and other Tales. 4s.

Essays, Critical and Imaginative. 4 vols., 16s.

The Noctes Ambrosianæ. 4 vols., 16s.

Homer and his Translators, and the Greek Drama. Crown 8vo, 4s.

WITHIN AN HOUR OF LONDON TOWN. Among Wild Birds and their Haunts. By "A SON OF THE MARSHES." *See page* 28.

WORSLEY.

Poems and Translations. By PHILIP STANHOPE WORSLEY, M.A. Edited by EDWARD WORSLEY. Second Edition, Enlarged. Fcap. 8vo, 6s.

Homer's Odyssey. Translated into English Verse in Spenserian Stanza. By P. S. Worsley. Third Edition. 2 vols. fcap., 12s.

Homer's Iliad. Translated by P. S. Worsley and Prof. Conington. 2 vols. Crown 8vo, 21s.

YATE. England and Russia Face to Face in Asia. A Record of Travel with the Afghan Boundary Commission. By Captain A. C. YATE, Bombay Staff Corps. 8vo, with Maps and Illustrations, 21s.

YATE. Northern Afghanistan; or, Letters from the Afghan Boundary Commission. By Major C. E. YATE, C.S.I., C.M.G. Bombay Staff Corps, F.R.G.S. 8vo, with Maps, 18s.

YOUNG. A Story of Active Service in Foreign Lands. Compiled from letters sent home from South Africa, India, and China, 1856-1882. By Surgeon-General A. GRAHAM YOUNG, Author of 'Crimean Cracks.' Crown 8vo, Illustrated, 7s. 6d.

YULE. Fortification: For the use of Officers in the Army, and Readers of Military History. By Colonel YULE, Bengal Engineers. 8vo, with Numerous Illustrations, 10s. 6d.

11/92.

www.ingramcontent.com/pod-product-compliance
Lightning Source LLC
Chambersburg PA
CBHW032135160426
43197CB00008B/649